MW01602797

How To Travel The World As A Vegan

By Maria Giurcan

This book is dedicated to my aunts Ana and Rosalia in Romania, for their kind invitation to visit them over a decade ago.

My desire to meet my paternal relatives for the first time side was stronger than my fear of flying.

Table of Contents

About Me

Maria - The "Vegan World Trekker"

My name is Maria, the "Vegan World Trekker". I blog about my global and domestic vegan travels, in addition to sharing vegan travel advice. My website and blog is found at www.veganworldtrekker.com.

My Story

I became vegetarian at the age of eight. I recall the exact moment. My 3rd grade teacher told us an animal story one day and at that moment it hit me - We eat living creatures for food but we don't have to do this! Fast forward to 2002, I attended a lecture with film presentation given on the topic of veganism. That presentation made me realize that once dairy cattle produce enough milk, they are then considered worthless and are slaughtered. Males are non-milk-producing, so are slaughtered also. Babies become veal calves. This revelation really touched my heart. Thus I became vegan from that day on!

Initially, I had a great fear of flying. However, in 1998 I was invited by my relatives to visit them in Romania. My desire to meet my relatives for the first time was stronger than my fear of flying! I am so glad that I accepted the opportunity to meet my family members. It was so thrilling to experience international landscapes, explore other cultures, and meet other peoples. I have been traveling across the globe ever since.

Purpose

The purpose of this book is to show vegans that it is possible to travel all over the world and find amazing dining options. This book does not attempt to describe the vegan dining situation in every country on the globe. It will attempt to cover the 70 or 80 countries most frequented by travelers, in addition to some up and coming holiday destinations such as Vietnam, Columbia, and Jordan. Many vegan travel issues are addressed.

Section 1

The first section of this book discusses vegan travel concerns and covers such topics as airport dining options, cruise/train/hotel dining for vegans, translating vegan meal requests in foreign languages, veggie-friendly tours, vegan coupon deals, vegan travel products, vegan shops, vegan accommodations, rest stop dining on highways, foods to bring on your trip, questions to ask international wait staff, and much more.

In addition, I provide my "best of" lists for restaurants across the globe, international bakeries, vegan-friendly souvenirs, and more.

Trip Preparation

The most important factor in preparing for a trip, any trip, is to do alot of research on the web. In addition to checking the basics such as safety and crime, independent traveler concerns, modes of transportation, local tours, accommodations, currency exchange, and sightseeing options, it is of utmost importance for vegans and vegetarians to research what kind of dining options are available at their destination. Are there vegetarian, vegan, or at least, veggie-friendly restaurants or cafes close to your hotel, close to the center of town, and close to your sightseeing activities? If not, are you in close proximity to any local markets or supermarkets to purchase staples such as deli sandwiches, salads, fruits, or soups? I research online for vegan bakeries, vegan donut shops, vegan ice cream shops, vegan pizza shops, vegan health food stores, and vegan clothing shops at my destination. These days, you can find pizza with soy cheese and soymilk-based gelatos and frozen yogurts.

I also conduct research on the web to determine what the national dishes are, what the local favorite foods are, and what the staples in the local diet are. Are there local beverages specific to this region? Are there popular indigenous cuisines that go back in time to the regions' ancestors? I then check the most popular web sites for vegetarian and vegan restaurants across the globe.

Another way to prepare for your travels is to bring your own meals including a vegan sandwich such as Tofurky (for eating at the airport), hummus, tabouleh, felafel rollup, vegan "beef jerky," trail mix, energy bars, fruit, salty snacks, and mixed nuts for the plane excursion and lengthy bus tours. You could even make homemade date walnut or chocolate chip trail mix bars to bring on the plane. In the event that you take a lengthy tour and the tour group dines at a restaurant with no vegan options, I advise you to bring oatmeal or dried "camping meals". You just need to add hot water. This meal is a great choice when a particular restaurant does not have vegan options. Packaged dry soups, veggie burgers, noodles or rice are also great to take along with you. Just add hot water and you have a hot, filling meal for the airport or tour.

Upon arrival at a destination, the individual traveller may want to visit a local bazaar or open-air market. Typically, you could purchase a sandwich, snack, beverage, or entire meal there. Seasoned travelers often comment that some of their best meals have been found at bazaars or street vendor stands. If you are fortunate enough to find one of these bazaars in your travels and they do indeed have vegetarian or vegan food, I suggest you purchase some items such as non-perishable sandwiches or snacks to carry with you for the remainder of your tour. It is always a good idea to be well-prepared. You may not know in advance if your next tour stop will bring you to a destination that is just as veggie-friendly. Stock up at the open-air market with light purchases for several days.

Vegan Dining on Trains

Travelers who journey by the inexpensive Euro Rail continental train or luxury trains such as the Asian Orient Express will be provided with dining facilities on board. The dining car restaurant will offer meal service. Special diet requests, such as "vegan" need to be made by contacting the train service anywhere from 24 hours to 72 hours in advance.

Vegan Dining on Cruise Ships

Many cruise lines offer either a vegan menu or have a few vegan options on their vegetarian menu. Others suggest that travelers request to meet with the chef when they arrive on board the ship. It is required that vegans request their vegan menu in advance, upon booking their trip by phone. Certain luxury cruise lines have specialty restaurants on board that may have a few vegan options.

Vegan Meals In Large, Chain Hotels

A number of large-scale hotel chains have a restaurant or two at their location. Many popular American hotel chains usually do not serve vegan entrees in their restaurants. Some larger, more luxurious, international hotels have several restaurants on their premises. These serve a variety of ethnic cuisines. In Cairo, Egypt, for example, I stayed at a large hotel that had three or four international cuisine restaurants in its lobby. I chose to dine at the Indian restaurant, as they were sure to have some vegan entrees on their menu!

Vegan Restaurant Research

Veggie-friendly Restaurants: (search the following websites to locate vegan or vegan-friendly restaurants in the country or city you are visiting)

www.happycow.net

www.ivu.org

www.vegeats.com/restaurants

www.vegdining.com

www.vegguide.org

www.euroveg.eu

www.veggieheaven.com

www.vegetarian-restaurants.net/International.htm

www.vrg.org/links/restaurant.htm

The above resources provide information regarding any restaurants or markets in your destination country, including the states in the USA. The results page will display keywords and symbols for the user to see if the options are vegetarian only, vegan, vegan-friendly, or even ovo/lacto-vegetarian. The complete street address and city will be displayed, in addition to phone numbers when available. You should be careful, however. There are times when a restaurant may be closed but the website has not been informed yet.

There are some chain restaurants such as Govinda's which are popular in many countries. Govinda's is always a safe bet for veggie-hungry travelers. They usually serve Indian cuisine. However, in certain countries such as Peru, they serve local, indigenous cuisine. I highly recommend them as good quality meals.

If you join VegDining ($15.95 or $11.95 if your local vegetarian society group is a member), you get discounts at vegetarian/vegan restaurants all over the USA and the world if they are part of the program. Lots of international restaurants join every week. You may also obtain a login on their website for a minimal cost per year. This entitles you to research global restaurants for information and reviews.

Vegan Mobile Apps

Traveling vegans now have the option of accessing information via mobile applications. Several vegan applications exist that will help vegans locate restaurants, find cruelty-free skincare, and assist with language translation while on vacation.

These applications can be downloaded to IPhones, Androids, and Palm cell phone devices. If the phone includes a international GSM SIM card, then these apps may be used while on holiday anywhere across the globe.

HappyCow.net provides a page with links from which these applications may be downloaded.
www.happycow.net/mobile.html

Be Nice To Bunnies – This mobile app from Peta.org helps travelers find cruelty-free haircare, cosmetics and skincare products, as well as other items.

http://itunes.apple.com/app/bnb/id3137849 33?mt=8

Cruelty-Free – This mobile app also helps travellers locate vegan cosmetics and skincare products.

http://itunes.apple.com/us/app/cruelty-free/id313825734?mt=8

VegOut - This application download from ITunes is for IPhone, Android, and palm devices. It helps you find vegetarian and vegan restaurants all over the world.

http://itunes.apple.com/app/vegout-vegetarian-restaurant/id301275521?mt=8

Veggie Passport – This guide helps travelers translate their dining needs in 33 languages. For the IPhone.

http://itunes.apple.com/app/veggie-passport/id306516080?mt=8

Vegan "Fast Food" Restaurants

I recently became aware of a wonderful, new concept in the vegan world: vegan "fast food" restaurants. Several of them exist across Europe. There is at least one in the United States also, right in New York City.

Foodswings is an all-vegan, fast food restaurant in the Brooklyn neighborhood of New York City. Diners can select from such items as chicken nuggets, buffalo wings, potato skins, nachos, sausage hero subs, burgers, hot dogs, fish n chips, tempeh rueben sandwiches, tofu "egg" sandwiches, and more! Of course, every item is vegan. It is the vegan version of classic, fast food fare that carnivores have been enjoying for years but for which vegans have been deprived until now.

For example, the hot dog is made of non-meat ingredients. They even serve some decadent desserts such as vegan coconut cake. Quite a few vegan soymilk shakes grace their menu as well. Each of the vegan items resembles their carnivorous counterparts. This is a great restaurant concept for former carnivores that are new to the vegan scene and for long time vegans too!

Foodswings: (www.foodswings.net)

Address:

295 Grand Street

Brooklyn, New York

Boston, MA now has a vegan diner of its own. "Veggie Galaxy" opened in September of 2011.

The diner is a throwback to the 1950's era with counter seating and booths. The menu includes comfort food such as veggie burgers, mac and cheese, seitan loaf, fries, and soymilk shakes and frappes. It will have an in-house bakery offering Boston cream pie, cakes, cookies, and other sweets.

The all-day breakfast includes pancakes, French toast, tofu scramble, and vegan omelettes.

It is not uncommon these days to find veggie-friendly restaurants that offer vegan BBQ. The sandwiches are typically seitan with a BBQ sauce. In various locations across the United States, Africa, and the Carribean Islands, vegans can feast upon "Ital" food. This Jamaican cuisine is vegan. For example, the vegetarian "Legassi Gardens" Bed&Breakfast in Accra, Ghana serves Ital meals to its guests.

There are several, vegan, fast food places in Europe as well. Vöner in Berlin, Germany boasts several fast food items on its menu. Diners may choose amongst several kinds of faux "meat" that is then sliced and placed into pita bread. Alongside the sandwich, patrons may have an order of cheesy fries. Other options here are seitan nuggets, fish n chips, or sandwich wraps. Desserts are offered as well.

Vöner (www.voener.de)

Address:
Boxhagener Straße 56
10245 Berlin, Germany

Another vegan fast food restaurant in Berlin is Vego Foodworld. Menu items include pizza, soy nuggets, burgers, and chips. They offer vegan milkshakes also.

Vego Foodworld (www.vego-foodworld.de)

Address:
Lychener Straße 63
10437 Berlin, Germany

Yoyo Foodworld is another vegan, "fast food" restaurant in Berlin. Their menu includes pizza, burgers, nuggets, spaghetti, "sausage", and other standard "fast food" fare. Dessert is offered as well.

Yoyo Foodworld (www.yoyofoodworld.de)

Address:
Gärtnerstr. 27
10245 Berlin-Friedrichshain, Germany

Belgium:

In Ghent, Belgium, one will find de Frietketel, a vegan "fast food" restaurant. They serve burgers, pot roast, meat balls, and other items in flavorful sauces.

de Frietketel

Address:
De Papegaaiestraat 89
Ghent, Belgium

England:

In Brighton and London, England proudly offers a vegan, fast food restaurant called Red Veg. They serve up vegan burgers, soywurst, hot dogs, fries, and more.

Red Veg

Address:

Brighton:
21 Gardner Street, Brighton, BN1 1UP
London:
95 Dean Street, London, W1V 5RB

It is well worth the effort to do an online search for vegan, "fast food" restaurants prior to any journey.

Vegan Food and Snacks for Your Trip

Vegan travel is not always easy. Sometimes it can be quite challenging! While websites like VegDining and HappyCow do a fantastic job helping travelers find vegan restaurants, the typical vegan traveler will probably encounter issues at the airport and during his or her vacation. Most airports do not have vegan options at their cafes. I actually run around and around each segment of the airport looking for something vegan-friendly to eat. Even the salads contain cheese at airport cafes. I typically am forced to buy a bag of trail mix or nuts or fruit or chips at the kiosks. I would like a hot meal or a sandwich! So in response to these problems, I realized it was time to be pro-active…time to bring the food I crave to eat. In addition, vegan travelers will often find that they do not always have dining options during their vacation tours. If they are on a group-organized, professional tour, the tour company will bring the group to a particular restaurant. You can ask the tour guide or waiter to find out if the chef would be willing to make a vegan meal for you. They usually will, but sometimes may not be able to do so because certain sauces or toppings have been pre-made.

Suggestions on what vegan foods to bring with you on your trip:
1. trail mix

2. date-nut bars, energy bars, etc

3. dried fruit

4. chips, pretzels, crackers, vegan "Tings"
http://www.gomaxgofoods.com/products-01.htm

5. vegan "faux beef" jerky

6. sandwiches with non-perishable ingredients for the short-term, airport meals (avocado, tomato, vegan cheese)

7. dry cereal or oatmeal cups (add hot water at airport or hotel for a filling breakfast).

8. dried, frozen packaged "camping meals" (add hot water). Outdoor goods companies such as Eastern Mountain Sports carry these dried meals packages. Perfect for your trip during times when there are no vegan cafes near to your hotel or tour group.
http://outdoorherbivore.com/about/
http://www.backpackerspantry.com/inventory.asp?ite mCategory=Entr%E9e&meatType=Vegetarian&portio nSize=2

9. vegan cookies

A. Enjoy Life - http://www.enjoylifefoods.com/our_foods/cookies.html

B. Liz Lovely Cookies - http://www.lizlovely.com/

C. Boston Cookies - http://www.bostoncookies.com/

10. sliced tofurky in pita bread rollup

11. packaged dried Asian noodle bowls. Vegan-friendly brands such as Amy's or Annie Chun's make Chinese noodle entrees, Pad Thai, Italian, and other noodle selections. Just add hot water at hotel or airport for a delicious, filling meal when no vegan dining options are to be found!

12. packaged vegan Indian specialties such as curries, chickpeas, rice, and eggplant dishes(liquid form). They would be best to eat at hotels or during bus tours. No cooking required and ready to serve! The TastyBite brand offers several packaged, pre-prepared Indian and Thai meals. These are lightweight and perfect to pack in luggage. http://www.tastybite.com/

13. dried soups. Dr. McDougall brand offers several vegan soups. These are also compact and lightweight and fit nicely into luggage. http://www.rightfoods.com/

14. bagels

The options above will ensure that you do not starve during your vegan travels and that you won't be running around the airport frantically to find meals as I have done in the past! These food items are also great to bring with you when you rent a car for a road trip.

Vegan Bars:

Pure Bar: www.thepurebar.com

Bumble Bar: www.bumblebar.com

Vega Bars: myvega.com/products/whole-food-energy-bar/features-benefits?gclid=CI3Bpb2GjKMCFUNf2godhStJbQ

www.veganbars.com

http://www.crispycatcandybars.com/

http://www.gomaxgofoods.com/products-01.htm

Vegan Gummy Bears:
store.veganessentials.com/organic-vegan-gummi-bears-p954.aspx

Vegan Snacks:
Sunfood - www.sunfood.com/Categories/1/raw-organic-snacks-and-treats.aspx

www.vegangiftshop.com/vegan_snacks.html

www.peta.org/accidentallyvegan/veganshoppingqs-snacks.asp?category=snacks

Vegan Candy:
www.naturalcandystore.com/category/vegan-candy

www.vegancandy.com

Vegan Chocolate:
Betty Lou's, Inc:
www.bettylousinc.com/products_diet.php?id=15
earthhopenetwork.net/natural_organic_chocolates.ht
m#vc

Vegan Jerky:
www.primalspiritfoods.com/products.php

Airports, Airlines, In-flight Meals

Very few airports have vegan dining options. Many airport cafes in the United States and abroad may have vegetarian options such as sandwiches with cheese, Mexican, pasta, salads, etc. Vegans may need to resort to airport kiosks for salads, chips, fruits, and nuts if they did not bring the vegan meal options from home that I suggested earlier. Much to my surprise, I found that the Salt Lake City airport has a bar with a few vegan options such as a vegan grain veggie burger and tofu scramble. We need more of these options, domestically and abroad! I've heard that this situation may be improving in airports such as Logan International in Boston, as a couple of the airport cafes are adding more vegan options. Internationally, there are a few airports with decent vegan dining.

Airlines do not typically provide vegan snacks. You should bring your own snacks for flights and while waiting for flights. At best, some snacks provided on board may be vegetarian such as cheese and crackers or mini-cookies. You should call the airlines and connecting flights to pre-order veggie-friendly meals. Some airlines, not all, provide vegan or vegetarian options. For vegans, I suggest the "Asian meal" which some airlines offer. This is usually a decent-tasting meal of brown rice with mixed vegetables and fruit for dessert. I always enjoy it. There are rarely breakfast choices for vegans, so please stock up on vegan snacks to bring with you. Some airlines do offer a vegan breakfast of bagels and fruit (check my airline meal link below). Verify that they use non-dairy butter and no cream cheese.

Also, the airlines that offer meals will do so during international flights. For domestic flights, it is best to dine at the airport or to bring something with you. Some airlines offer snack packs for purchase during longer, domestic flights. For example, United Airlines offers an organic snack pack, perfect for vegans that includes pretzels, hummus, olives, sesame sticks, and crackers.

Airline Meals by category (vegan,vegetarian,etc): www.vrg.org/travel/airtravel.htm

www.happycow.net/travel/air_travel.html

www.airlinesmeals.net/indexSpecialmeals.html

These days there are several choices for budget-conscious travelers. Some of the low-cost, popular airlines around include Southwest Airlines, JetBlue, Spirit Airlines, and AirTran.

One of the issues on these inexpensive airlines is that they do not serve meals, regardless of the length of the flight. This holds true for both vegans and carnivores alike. However, they do offer several snacks. Some of the budget airlines offer free snacks. Others charge a small fee. Most of the snacks are not vegan. It is important to read the labels for some items such as the crackers to determine if they are made with butter. Bagel packages must be checked for ingredients such as eggs. The safe bets for vegans are the raisins, nuts, and pretzels.

Vegan-Friendly Airlines

United States:

American Airlines

Continental Airlines

Delta Airlines

United Airlines

US Airways

Europe and Canada:

Air Canada

British Airways

Aer Lingus

Virgin Atlantic

Lufthansa

Al Italia

Turkish Airlines

KLM Airlines

Air Malta

Australia and New Zealand:

Qantas Airways

Air New Zealand

Asia:

Indian Airlines

Cathay Pacific

Malaysia Airlines

Qatar Airways

Singapore Airlines

Vietnam Airlines

Vegan-Friendly Airports

The following USA airports were rated the "Top Five" in the country, for providing healthy, vegan-friendly dining options:
1. Salt Lake City – Squatter's Pub (www.squatters.com/) serves tofu scramble and veggie burgers
2. Dallas/Fort Worth – 360 Gourmet (vegan burritos), Blue Bamboo Express, Cool River Cafe, UFood Grill (felafel roll-up)
3. Chicago O'Hare – Burrito Beach, Cafe Zoot, Cibo Express, Salad Works, Goose Island Brewing (marinated portobello panini) and a few other cafes offering vegan sandwiches.
4. Los Angeles – Sushi Boy, Creative Croissants
5. Albuquerque, New Mexico – Several cafes offer vegan portobello wraps and a few other options.

Other Vegan-Friendly Airports in the USA:

Logan Airport in Boston has a restaurant called "Boston Back Bay Cafe" which serves Vegan Pad Thai, Italian, Vegan Dumplings, and Vegan Udon Noodles. Other options at Logan are French Meadow Bakery & Cafe and UFood Grill.

Miami – Sushi Bar, Bongos

NYC JFK – French Meadow; NY LaGuardia – Cibo Express

Detroit – Mediterranean Grill, Sora, National Coney Island Express, Earl Of Sandwich, Mushashi
Minneapolis – 360 Gourmet, French Meadow Baker & Cafe (vegan grilled Reuben sandwich)

San Francisco – Harbor Village Kitchen (veggie curry&rice), Max's The Greek

Phoenix – Home Turf Bar, Yoshi's Asian Grill, Chili's Too (black bean burger)

Houston – Lotus Express, Charlie's Express, Houston To Go

Orlando – McCoys, Qdoba, Cibo Express

Baltimore/Washington International Airport – Silver Diner (portobello vegetarian stir-fry with tofu, veggies, and wheat noodles), Zona Mexicana – veggie burritos

Ronald Reagan Washington National Airport – Cosi, Cibo

Washington Dulles International Airport – Moe's Grill & Bar

The following international airports have been noted as offering vegan-friendly dining:

International Airports:
Mexico City – 100% Natural
London Heathrow – Wagamamas (vegan options)

Brisbane, Australia – Noodle Box

Zurich, Switzerland – Asian Place

Vegan Questions to Ask in Restaurants

As every vegan knows, there is a list of ingredients we can not consume and food preparation steps that need to be followed to a "T". If you find yourself dining with your tour group at a non-vegan establishment there are questions you must ask the wait staff.

Remember to ask the waiter at your restaurant the following questions:

1. Does the entree contain dairy (yogurt, milk, cheese, butter), eggs/egg whites, or honey?

2. Is the food cooked in vegetable oil or butter?

3. For beans, rice, and couscous, ask the waiter if it has been cooked in lard, beef fat, pork fat, or chicken broth.

4. Especially in Asian countries, ask if they use separate pots and pans to cook or stir-fry the veggie dish or if it has been transferred to the same pan which had previously contained meat. Sometimes they only rinse the pan with water (no soaps) before using it again to cook veggies.

5. Ask if there is any fish product (or fish sauce, anchovies) or chicken in your meal. For whatever reason, certain cultures do not consider seafood or poultry to be living creatures such as mammals are. They assume that these are vegetarian.

6. Is the pasta made with eggs?

Your tour guide or your "Vegan Passport" guide book can assist with the language translations

The water is not safe to consume in various parts of the world including some Central and South American countries, some Asian countries, and some African countries. Many people have become ill from drinking the water. Vegans should especially beware. Vegetables should be peeled and cooked. Raw vegetables and salads should be avoided during travel, especially in regions known for contaminated water. Ice cubes should never be used in beverages. Fruit juices and any beverage should not contain the local water. It is best to drink bottled, canned or hot beverages.

Ordering Vegan Meals in Other Languages

The next thing to be concerned with is how to order a meal or beverage at your destination, if the native language is not English. One of the best solutions may be to enroll in an adult education language course in the primary language of your destination country. It is important to educate yourself regarding the names of vegetables, rice, grains, beans, desserts, pastas, and beverages so that you may order a variety of breakfast, lunch and dinner options each day of your visit. Another great option is to purchase "The Vegan Passport". This is a guide book that contains various important phrases such as "I am vegan or a strict vegetarian" in approximately 95% of the world's languages.

There are also travel pocket guide's such as "Point it!" containing photos of very important travel vocabulary items such as transportation, accommodation options, and food items. Just point at what you wish to eat.

Translation Guides

"Vegan Passport" – translations for vegan food phrases in 95% of the world's languages.

"Point It!" – pocket guide containing photos of food and beverages (among other travel-related items).

This is great for vegan travelers who do not speak the language of their destination country. Just point at the veggie in the guidebook and the waiter will understand what you wish to order. It will make vegan travel easy!

IVU website (International Vegetarian Union) – www.ivu.org/phrases/

This site lists phrases such as "I do not eat eggs, cheese, or butter" in many world languages.

Translation Tools

Some of you may own a copy of the "Vegan Passport" which can translate phrases such as "I am vegan" or "I do not eat butter, cheese, and eggs". Others may have purchased the "Point It!" guide so that you can point to a photo of a vegetable you would like for dinner. This makes it easy for a waiter to understand you if you do not speak their language.

However, there still may be times when you wish to relay a lengthier message to the waiter or chef. You may need to describe an entire meal or ask particular questions regarding broth, lard, or food preparation.

In these situations when you wish to translate a substantial amount of information, there are two great tools you can use!

The first is called Yahoo! BabelFish:
babelfish.yahoo.com

You just need to enter the text you would like translated, then select the "To" and "From" languages. You may want to consider what you might need to translate before you leave on your journey. You can also utilize the computer at home and print out the translated information. The other option is to utilize the computer at your hotel or internet cafe at your destination. Either way, you are never at a loss to translate any statement or question you may have for the wait staff at the restaurants in which you dine during your travels.

The other online translation tool is Google Translate

http://translate.google.com/

Vegan Phrases in Popular Languages

French:
"I am vegan" – Je suis vegen
I do not eat meat, fish, chicken – Je ne mange pas de viande, de poisson, de poulet
I do not eat cheese or eggs – Je ne mange pas des frommage, des oeufs
I do not drink milk – Je ne bois pas de lait

German:
"I am vegan" – Ich bin Veganer
I do not eat meat, fish, chicken – Ich esse kein Fleisch, auch kein Huhn (und keinen Fisch).
I do not eat eggs, milk, or cheese – Ich esse keine Eier, Milch oder Käse.

Spanish:
"I am vegan" -Yo soy vegano (a)
I do not eat meat, fish, chicken – Yo no como el carne , el pescado, el pollo
I do not eat eggs, milk, cheese -Yo no como los huevos, la leche, el queso

Italian:
"I am vegan" – Sono vegano (a)
I do not eat meat, fish, chicken - Non mangio carne, ne pollo o pesce
I do not drink milk – non bevo il latte
I do not eat butter, cheese, eggs, or honey – Non mangio il burro, il formaggio, le uova, o il miele

Chinese(Mandarin for Beijing travelers):
wo chi su. – I am a vegetarian
wo bu chi rou, wo chi shu cai. – I don't eat meat, I eat vegetable
wo bu chi yu – I don't eat fish
wo bu chi ji – I don't eat chicken
wo bu chi dan – I don't eat egg
wo bu chi niunai – I don't drink milk

Arabic:
Ana Nabatee (I am vegetarian [male]
Ana Nabateeya (I am vegetarian) [female]
Mish Akool Lahma walla Ferekh khalis (I don't eat meat or chicken at all)

Hindi:
Main maas-machhli nahin khata/khati (masculine/feminine) hoon. (I do not eat meat [includes poultry] or fish.)

Vegetarian and Vegan Travel Guides

Guides to vegetarian and vegan restaurants and accommodations:

"Vegetarian Europe" by Alex Bourke
This book was written several years ago. It can currently be purchased online.

"Vegetarian and Organic Paris" by Laure Goldbright
This book was written several years ago. It can currently be purchased online.

"Vegetarian London" by Alex Bourke
This book was written several years ago. It can currently be purchased online.

"Scotland The Green" by Jackie Redding
This book was written several years ago. It can currently be purchased online.

"The New Spain : Vegan & Vegetarian Restaurants" by Jean-Claude Juston

"Vegetarian Italy" by the Italian Vegetarian Association

"Guide to Vegetarian Restaurants in Israel" by Max Weintraub

"Vegetarian Journal's Guide to Natural Foods Restaurants in the U.S. And Canada" by the Vegetarian Resource Group

The following guides reveal vegan dining and accommodation information covering the globe:

"The Vegetarian Traveler" by Jed Civic – Where to atay If you are vegetarian, vegan

"The Vegetarian Traveler" by Bryan Geon – Where to eat in over 200 countries

"Vegan a Go Go" by Sarah Kramer – A cookbook and survival manual for vegans on the go

Guide Books:
"The Traveler's Diet" by Peter Greenberg – How to eat healthy in flight and on vacation

Vegan and Vegetarian Vacations

Vegetarian and vegan travel agencies offer holidays for like-minded people. A vegetarian or vegan meal is always provided. Sometimes the trip includes other veggie-friendly activities such a vegan cooking class or volunteer time at an animal sanctuary. The following travel companies run vegan or vegetarian tours or vacations:

Vegetarian and Vegan Holidays:

Veg Voyages www.vegvoyages.com

Green Earth Travel www.vegtravel.com

Vegi Ventures www.vegiventures.com
Vegetarian Vacations www.vegetarian-vacations.com/index.html
Responsible Travel www.responsibletravel.com/TripSearch/Special%20int erest/Activity100208.htm

Vegan Cruises:
A Taste Of Health www.atasteofhealth.org/vegan-cruise.htm

Vegan Camp:

www.vegancamp.co.uk

Veggie Festivals:

www.vegetarianguides.co.uk/calendar/index.shtml

Woofing:

WWoof (www.wwoof.org) refers to a worldwide network of organizations which links volunteers to organic farms. The volunteers provide help and in return the hosts offer food, accommodations and opportunities to learn about organic farming.

Vegan Dining on Cruise Lines

Several cruise lines these days offer vegan menus or vegan options on their vegetarian menus. Some may offer one vegan choice on their typical menu. International cuisine is becoming more popular on cruise ships. Tempeh, seitan, and tofu dishes can even be found sometimes on cruise line menus! Thai, Italian, Indian, or Mediterranean meals may be great choices for vegans.

Usually, the vegan menu must be requested in advance upon arrival on board the ship. The "specialty restaurants" of the cruise lines can usually prepare a vegan option upon request. The ship buffet stations typically have a vast array of fruits, vegetables and salads. The chef may be able to prepare some of the vegetables without butter or other dairy products, if you ask. Room service on most cruise lines offers salads and veggie burgers. Vegans need to inquire if the brand of veggie burger contains egg yolk. It is always a good idea for vegans to bring some of their own food from home also.

Royal Caribbean, Celebrity, Holland America, Norwegian, Princess, Costa, and Disney offer veggie options during their BBQ beach excursions on their own private Caribbean islands. Some of these cruise lines will prepare special bagged lunches for travelers to take with them during shore excursions, as many Caribbean ports do not have vegan restaurants.

On small cruise lines, travelers may meet directly with the chef to request special vegan meals. The Nile River cruise ship from Aswan to Luxor, Egypt has a sit down restaurant on board where travelers can select what they would like to eat from the large buffet. There are not many vegan options available at the buffet stations. However, vegans will not starve. The staples of freshly baked pita bread and ful (fava beans) are filling. The tour guide may speak to the chef in order to prepare some vegetables which are cooked in oil, instead of with dairy products.

A Taste Of Health Holistic Cruises

A Taste Of Health holistic cruises offer all-vegan trips. The cuisine on board includes vegan, macrobiotic, and raw foods. Travelers may also take vegan cooking classes on board, participate in yoga or meditation, or attend seminars given by top vegan or raw food speakers and nutritionists.

Royal Caribbean

Travelers should request vegan menu options in advance. You should speak to the head waiter as soon as you board the ship. Indian meals are usually an option.

Carnival Cruise Lines

Carnival has a special vegan menu in their restaurant. Travelers should request vegan meals in advance, when they arrive on board. This menu will be served to you for the length of your stay.

Norwegian Cruise Lines

Norwegian offers vegan options when requested in advance. Please contact the cruise line for more information. When booking the cruise by phone, ask to speak with the Group Event Coordinator upon arrival on board. The coordinator will schedule a meeting between you and the ship's chef. The chef will prepare vegan meals based on your discussion.

Windstar Cruise Lines

Windstar does not have a specific vegan menu. However, guests may request to meet with the chef on board. The chef will then prepare a vegan version of the vegetarian options available, based on your needs.

Celebrity Cruise Lines

Celebrity Cruise Lines offers a full vegan menu. It needs to be requested by calling Celebrity prior to your trip. A couple of the Celebrity ships offer raw foods.

Princess

Princess offers vegan options when requested by phone, in advance. Please contact the cruise line for more information.

Holland America

Holland America offers vegan options when requested by phone, in advance. Please contact the cruise line for more information. Special meals can be requested by calling the Ship Services Department 60 days prior to your trip.

Vegan Dining on Train Excursions

Many travelers choose to take train excursions to their destinations. Each continent and country providing rail service gives vacationers varying levels of comfort and amenities on the tracks. There are simplistic, inexpensive trains and luxury trains providing the utmost in care. Trains that carry passengers for lengthy journeys do provide meal services in their on board restaurant or cafe dining car. Sleeper car trains also provide meal service. Most of the luxury, long distance, and sleeper car trains provide special diet meals upon request. Vegans may request this. The request must be made at least 72 hours in advance.

United States

Amtrak: www.amtrak.com

Europe

Euro Rail:

The Euro Rail train service provides travel to many European countries from north to south. Their website is www.eurail.com

Europe, USA, UK Train information
www.railplus.com.au

Euro Railways: Many European destinations

www.eurorailways.com/corp

Peru

Peru Rail:
www.perurail.com/web/tper/tper_a2a_home.html

Hiram Bingham: (to Machu Picchu)
www.perurail.com/web/tper/tper_luxurytravel_introduc
tion.html

Turkey

www.tcdd.gov.tr/tcdding/index.htm

India

India Railways: www.indianrail.gov.in

Thailand

www.seat61.com/Thailand.htm#Bangkok%20to%20C
hiang%20Mai

Southeast Asia

Orient Express: www.luxury-trains.co.uk/eastern_oriental_express.htm

Australia

The Ghan, Indian Pacific, The Overland: www.gsr.com.au

Rail Australia: www.railaustralia.com.au

Kenya

East Africa Shuttles: www.eastafricashuttles.com/train.htm

South Africa

ROVOS Rail: www.luxury-trains.co.uk/rovos_rail.htm

Blue Train: www.luxury-trains.co.uk/blue_train.htm

Vegan Dining at Hotel Chain Restaurants

Travelers do not always have the time to go to a restaurant for breakfast, lunch, or dinner when their next tour is coming up shortly. You never really know how long it will take to be served in a restaurant or how long it will take the meal to be prepared. It is quicker to eat in your hotel's restaurant to save commute time. That said, most hotels do not offer vegan options.

For breakfast, it is usually not much of a problem as fruit salad, toast with jam or a bagel (ask if egg coating on it) are common breakfast fare at any hotel. However, for lunch and dinner, vegan travelers do not have an easy time at the typical hotel chain restaurant. It is fairly common for hotel restaurants to offer pasta dishes or veggie burgers to vegan diners. However, vegans will need to verify with the waiter or chef that these meals do not contain eggs or egg yolks.

Hilton Hotels

The Hilton Hotel chain seems to be one of the best for vegan diners! Their worldwide locations have different restaurants on site within their hotels. Some of their locations have vegetarian meals which can be requested as vegan. Many of these restaurants do offer vegan options on their menu. For example, their hotel at Heathrow Airport in London offers vegan options at each of their on-site restaurants. Hilton's Kerala, India location offers good vegan dining also.

Ritz Carlton Hotel

The Ritz is an elegant, luxury hotel. Their various locations have several, different restaurants on site. Most of them serve veggie-friendly meals. Vegans will find quite a few selections ranging anywhere from Asian fare to tofu dishes.

Marriott Hotel

The Marriott Hotel chains have several restaurants on site. Some of them are buffet-style cafes with pre-made food at their buffet stations. Vegans may ask the waiters which items are made without dairy or eggs. Their sit-down restaurants have a few vegetarians items which may be prepared vegan upon speaking with the chef. They are accommodating to vegan requests.

Crowne Plaza

Some of the Crowne Plaza restaurants serve limited vegetarian options. A few of the vegetable side dishes or stir fry may be requested as vegan without the butter.

Radisson

This chain does not offer much vegan food or even many vegetarian entrees. However, some of their USA locations offer veggie burgers or pasta made without eggs. Vegans should request these. Some of their international locations offer more interesting vegan fare. For example, their Aruba location has a couple of restaurants offering a vegan option. One is called Gilligans and offers Mediterranean Vegetable Wrap which is vegan. The other restaurant on site is called Sunset Grille and offers a grilled portobello sandwich.

Another example is their Sydney, Australia location. It has several vegetable side dishes on the menu. Vegans may ask the chef to prepare them without butter or cheese.

Doubletree
This hotel does not offer many vegetable selections. Some locations offer veggie burgers. Vegans should inquire if they contain eggs.

Holiday Inn
There are not many vegetarian or vegan dishes at most locations. However, pasta dishes may be vegan. The waiters can tell you if the dishes contain eggs. International locations, such as in Asian countries have more vegan offerings. The Holiday Inn in Beijing, China actually has a vegan restaurant "Pure Lotus" in their location.

Sheraton
There are not many vegetarian or vegan dishes at most locations. Sangkee Noodle House restaurant is located in the lobby of the Philadelphia Sheraton. Vegans may find suitable meals there. Some of their international locations, such as Hawaii or Thailand offer a greater selection of vegan fare such as noodles or mixed vegetable dishes.

Wyndham
There are not many vegetarian or vegan dishes at most locations. Some international locations, such as Mexico have several ethnic restaurants on site. These may be suitable for vegans.

In summary, large hotel chains still need to include a greater number of vegan options at their restaurants and worldwide locations. While several large chain hotel restaurants do offer vegan options, there are an even greater number of them which only offer vegan options in a few of their international locations. The chain hotel industry does appear to be becoming more vegan friendly as time goes by.

Several years ago, PETA wrote a "Vegetarian Report Card Hotels". It made mention of the various hotel chains and how accommodating their restaurants were to vegetarians and vegans.

www.goveg.com/f-hotels06.asp.

Vegan Bakeries, Sweets, and Ice Cream

Let's discuss what kinds of vegan food products you should research online prior to your international journeys.

Whenever I travel, I first go online to the VegDining.com or HappyCow.net websites to locate vegan or vegan-friendly restaurants in my destination city. I enter the name of the country or city to return a list of vegan/vegan-friendly restaurants. As you check each of the returned websites, you should also notice which ones serve a vegan brunch.

I also do an online search for vegan ice cream, gelato, donuts, cupcakes, snacks, candy, and chocolate. Basically, I bring up google, then enter the keywords "vegan" +"ice cream" +"Montreal" (for example). Google then returns links to any shops in Montreal (for example) that may serve vegan ice cream. I do similar searches for vegan cupcakes and so forth.

You would be surprised at just how many vegan food shops you may find globally!! For example, it is not a difficult task to find vegan ice cream all over North America, Europe, and Australia. However, it is difficult to find in South America. Vegan gelato is also sold across the USA and Europe. Though you may not always find an ice cream shop that is completely vegan, you may find an ice creamerie that offers five or six vegan varieties. Such is the case at Meu Meu in Montreal, Canada.

Vegan donut shops are sprouting up at various locations as well. The donut shops are not typically as common as vegan ice creameries. However, it is well worth the online research if you find such a tasty treat during your travels!!

I also search online for vegan bakeries at my destination country and city. Again, the search may find bakeries which sell some vegan goods, not necessarily a completely vegan bakery. My next step is to specifically do a search for vegan cupcakes in that city.

After completing this online research, I feel well-prepared to explore the vegan scene in any international city that I visit!

When your day of sightseeing adventures is complete and you've finished eating a delicious meal, you will most likely crave a vegan dessert! Fortunately, more and more vegan bakeries are opening worldwide (in addition to vegan restaurants serving a few vegan desserts such as cakes or pies).

I have compiled the following list of some vegan bakeries and vegan ice cream shops from all over the world.

Europe:

Nottingham, England:
The Screaming Carrot (www.screamingcarrot.co.uk)

42 Foxhill Road

Berlin, Germany:

Ufa Fabrik (www.ufafabrik.de)

Viktoriastr. 10-18
12105 Berlin / Tempelhof

Copenhagen, Denmark:

Det Rene Braud (www.xn--detrenebrd-8cb.dk)

Rosenvaengets Alle 17

2100 Kobenhavn 0

Stockholm, Sweden:

Starrva Bakery (www.sattvabageri.se)

Krukmakargatan 27a - 11851 Stockholm

Budapest, Hungary:
Reform Cukrasz (www.reformcukrasz.hu)

3rd district Kiskorona utca 8

Madrid, Spain:
La Chocolateria
C/Barbieri 15

Rome, Italy:
Blue Ice (vegan gelato options)
Via Sistina, 122

Florence, Italy:
Gelateria Dei Neri (some vegan options)
Via dei Neri, 22r

Asia:

Bangkok, Thailand:
Les Marg Bakery
Sukaphiban 1 Road (Bangkae)

Seoul, Korea:
Sticky Fingers Bakery (www.stickyfingers.co.kr)

Tokyo,Japan:
Der Akkord (www.der-akkord.jp/english.htm)

5-45-5 Jingumae, Shibuya-ku

Australia:

Melbourne, Australia:
Nelly's Vegan Bakery

www.veganbakery.com.au/Nellys_Vegan_Bakery/Wel
come.html

New Zealand:
Mamata Bakery
401 Richmond Rd, Grey Lynn

Montreal, Canada:

Meu Meu Ice Creamerie (some vegan flavors)

4458 Rue Saint-Denis

ShiShi Desserts (many varieties of vegan cupcakes)

7700 St Hubert

United States

New York City:

Babycakes Bakery (vegan cupcakes, pastries)

248 Broome St

Seattle, WA:

MightYo Donuts

2110 North 55th Street

Las Vegas, NV:

Ronald's Donuts

4600 Spring Mountain Road

Studio City, CA:

KindKreme (vegan ice cream)

3701 Cahuenga Blvd

Portland, OR:

Sweetpea Bakery (Vegan cakes, cupcakes, cookies)

1205 SE Stark Street

Manchester, Connecticut:

Divine Treasures (Vegan chocolate shop. They sell vegan ice cream treats also.)
http://www.divinetreasureschocolates.com/

Middlesex Turnpike West, #404

Pawtucket, Rhode Island:

Wildflour Bakery (vegan bakery)

http://www.wildflourveganbakerycafe.com/

727 East Avenue

Providence, Rhode Island:

Like No Udder (vegan ice cream)

http://www.like-no-udder.com/

This all-vegan ice cream truck drives around Providence, Rhode Island and may also be found at veggie-friendly festivals in Massachusetts.

Washington, DC:

Sticky Fingers Bakery

http://www.stickyfingers.com

1370 Park Road NW

Burlington, VT (Lake Champlain region):

Sabertooth Bakery

http://sabertoothbakery.blogspot.com/

Burlington, VT

This vegan bakery is actually a hot pink pushcart pulled by a bicycle. The owner rides the bicycle to downtown Burlington and displays the vegan baked goods on top of the cart.

Health Food Stores and All-Vegan Shops

HappyCow (like other vegan restaurant search sites) also returns a list of health food stores that carry vegan foods or vegan products. Whenever you would like a vegan meal or snack for your hotel room or for your lengthy bus tours, or souvenirs to take home with you, a visit to one of these international health food stores is a nice convenience. Some countries have all vegan natural food shops. Other shops may offer some vegan goods. One may purchase soy products, faux "meats", vegan cheeses, vegan ice cream, vegan baked goods, produce, and much more. These shops are plentiful in many parts of the world, especially in North America and Europe.

There is a vegan convenience store rumoured to be opening soon in New York City. Vegan Bodega (www.veganbodega.com) will be the first, all-vegan grocery store in this very vegan-friendly city. They plan on offering local products, as well as items that are new or difficult to find elsewhere.

Orlando, Florida is home to a vegan market called "Artichoke Red" (http://www.artichokered.com/). They sell vegan foods, pet products, cosmetics, body care items, cleaning products, aromatherapy, and teas.

The final research I do prior to my trip is to locate vegan shops. There are retail outlets internationally that sell vegan clothing, t shirts, vegan shoes, vegan skincare products, vegan bedding, vegan logo items, and so forth.

Examples are the "Secret Society Of Vegans" in London (www.secretsocietyofvegans.co.uk), "Vega Life" shop in Amsterdam (www.vega-life.nl) and the "Vegan Pride" shop in Sao Paulo, Brazil (www.veganpride.com).

Viva Granola Vegan Store (www.vivagranolaveganstore.ca) is located in Montreal, Canada. They sell vegan foods, skincare, clothing, cosmetics, jewelry, vegan books, pet supplies, vegan supplements, and much more.

Vegan-Friendly Accommodations

As you are well aware, many times during your travels you may be staying at a hotel or inn which does not provide vegan meals in their on-site cafe. Sometimes, a vegan-friendly restaurant is not even within walking distance. This may present an issue if you need to meet a tour group and do not have time to get to a restaurant. You may also be spending your holiday in a city which is not very veggie-friendly either.

There are quite a few countries in several continents which have veggie-friendly bed & breakfasts or inns. Some of them are advertised as vegetarian. However, a percentage of their restaurant menu is vegan. That portion of the menu may be anywhere from 10% to 90% vegan. Still there are other Bed and breakfasts which are 100% vegan.

The vast majority of these inns are located in rural settings, away from the hustle and bustle of city life, but close to nature. A few of them such as the one in Edinburgh, Scotland are located in the city, close to tourist attractions. Veggie-friendly inns are located in Mexico, Costa Rica, Ghana, The Gambia, Australia, New Zealand, India, Peru, Bali, Germany, Scotland, England, France, Austria, and other parts of Europe.

Another benefit (besides the vegan meals) of staying at these inns or B&Bs is that some of them offer many benefits such as yoga, meditation, community service projects, cooking classes, and much more.

They typically have a vegan-friendly, eco-friendly, nature-loving, inner peace vibe to them.

There are quite a few retreat centers and spas all over the world which focus on a weekend or week long program of healthy mind, body, and spirit workshops. The other wonderful thing about these retreat centers is that they offer vegan friendly meals! Some of them focus on raw foods. At a few of these centers, vegan meals must be requested. However, they are indeed provided to the guests that ask for them.

They offer programs in meditation, raw foods, relationships, spirituality, nutrition, maintaining a healthy body, or inner healing. Some even offer workshops on music and dance. Several vegan travel resources online will provide links for finding these retreat centers.

There are inns and Bed and Breakfast accommodations all over the world which cater to vegetarians and vegans. They usually provide a vegan breakfast. If the inn is vegan, then the bedding and pillows they provide will not be made of any animal product such as wool, silk, down, or feathers. The inn may also have a cafe on site which serves vegetarian or vegan lunch and dinner.

Vegan Bed and Breakfast Inns and Other Vegan-Friendly Accommodations:

www.vrg.org/links/vacation.htm

www.theveganlife.com/companies/bed-breakfasts.html

www.happycow.net/travel/bb_retreats.html

www.vegetarianusa.com/vacationmapworld2000.html

Legassi Gardens Bed & Breakfast in Accra, Ghana offers vegan breakfasts and made-to-order vegan "Ital" meals. The inn can also arrange for travelers to volunteer for service projects at orphanages or helping locals with organic farming, participate in local language or drumming lessons, or sign up for local tours.

There is a wonderfully unique concept gaining popularity in the travel world. It is known as couchsurfing (www.couchsurfing.org).

This phenomenon allows domestic and international travelers to stay at someone's home or apartment for free during their travels! There are people all over the world who offer up rooms in their homes for brief periods to international travelers. Both parties benefit from meeting others from different cultures. Over 200 countries are included in this program. Approximately two million travelers have enjoyed the benefits of couchsurfing!

It is a non-profit site and free to join. Users can choose to be verified. This way you will feel safer about the host's identity. The site even contains a "Tips" section to provide you with valuable information on how to be a host and how to be a couchsurfer. In addition, it includes references and vouchers on the host to insure your safety. Members may also post comments regarding scammers.

New users can create a profile, login, search for rooms in their country of choice and review the host references and testimonials of previous couchsurfers! All in all, it appears to be a safe, inexpensive way to travel across the globe. Since the accommodations are free, it leaves cash for vegan dining.

Also, because it does not include city tours or such, vegan travelers are not forced to dine at non-veggie friendly establishments as may have been necessary as part of a large tour group. You are free to dine at vegan restaurants of your choice!

Travelers may also search the couchsurfing site for hosts that are vegan. There are couchsurfing groups and subgroups. Members can join vegan subgroups and post messages regarding the vegan dining at their destination country. This will benefit the traveler twofold. The vegan host may provide valuable information on the vegan dining scene in their country and they may likely take their guest to one of their favorite vegan restaurants in town.

The "Vegan Around The World Network" (http://www.veganaroundtheworldnetwork.com) website is a resource for vegans to connect based on various commonalities such location, hobbies, cooking, and so forth. This is accomplished through message boards and discussion forums. Members sign up for free then create their bio and join the various groups that they choose based on interest. One of the newer forums is a vegan-based, couchsurfing group. Vegan members can post a message to let others know where they are travelling and on which dates, in hopes that another vegan in that destination will host them in their home or apartment. It is a great opportunity to get information about local vegan restaurants and to make vegan friends across the globe. The host member may even show you around their city or cook vegan meals for you.

Vegan Meals During Camping Trips

Whether you camp in the USA or abroad, you may have concerns about the kinds of foods you should bring with you as a vegan. Across the globe there are health food stores carrying vegan food items. Websites such as HappyCow.net list those stores for each destination country or city. When you need certain groceries, run out of some items, or need particular foods to be as fresh as possible, these health food stores should be a mandatory stop during your travels. There are certain staple foods that vegans should pack in their cooler for their camping trip.

Some of the following ideas will provide you with a nutritious and delicious food experience during your stay at the campsite.

Vegan Breakfast Foods:
Packaged oatmeal. You just add hot water.
Muesli. Add soymilk.
Scrambled tofu with veggies (green peppers, onions, broccoli, tomatoes, and herbs)
Vegan faux sausage
Vegan muffins
Fruit salads
Packaged vegan pancake mixes
Granola. Add soymilk.
Toast and jam

Vegan Lunch Foods:

Veggie faux chicken or beef
Packaged soup cups. Some brands include Nile
Spice and Spice Hunter.
Tofurky sandwich with vegan cheese
Avocado sandwich in pita bread
Hummus, tabbouleh, or baba ganoush in pita bread
Peanut butter sandwich
Veggie dogs. Grill them on BBQ.

Vegan Dinner Foods:
Packaged Indian meals (curries, eggplant, potatoes,
lentils, spinach, etc). A popular brand is Tasty Bite.

Packaged Thai or Asian meals including rice or
noodle dishes. A popular brand is Annie Chuns.

Veggie burgers with whole grains
Couscous, quinoa, bulgur
Whole wheat or rice flour pasta

Faux meats such as vegan chicken or vegan beef.
Tofu cubes or TVP to grill.

Packaged falafel mix. A popular brand is Fantastic
Foods.

Potatoes or corn on the cob to BBQ

Vegetables that can be put on a skewer to BBQ.
Some good choices are zucchini, carrots, squash,
peppers, and onions.

Freeze-dried, packaged, camping meals can be purchased online or from sporting goods stores such as Eastern Mountain Sports or REI. The packages are marked as vegetarian or vegan. Stores that sell the items, such as REI, also have a brochure containing a "V" next to the items that are vegan. Some of the meals may include rice, beans, pastas, curries and vegetable stews. Breakfast foods such as oatmeal with dried soymilk are sold by some of the vendors. All that is needed is some hot water to add to the meals. The packages are lightweight and easy to fit into luggage.

The following brands offer vegan, freeze-dried, packaged, camping meals:

Outdoor Herbivore – www.outdoorherbivore.com

Backpacker's Pantry – www.backpackerspantry.com

Mary Janes Farm - http://shop.maryjanesfarm.org

Snacks:
Fruit
Trail mix
Vegan cookies

Raisins

Nuts

Seeds

Rice cakes

Soy crisps

Fruit rollups

Vegan bars

Vegan S'mores made with dark chocolate, vegan marshmallows or soy whipped cream, and vegan graham crackers.

Vegan Ski Trips

Ski areas have typically presented many problems for vegans. That seems to no longer be the case. Just a few years ago, vegans could only count on finding a bag of potato chips or a piece of fresh fruit at a ski lodge. In just the past couple of years, ski lodges have started to offer more vegan-friendly options.

Several ski areas in New England sever vegan chilli at their mountain base lodge. Ski resort towns offer an eclectic array of restaurants and cafes serving ethnic cuisine. Many choices abound for vegans. Indian, Mexican and Thai restaurants now dot the landscape of these ski areas.

It is not uncommon for inns and bed and breakfast accommodations to offer at least one vegan option on their menus.

For example, there is a particular ski region in the state of Vermont which publishes a brochure containing a compilation of the nearby dining options. It even includes a column for vegan-friendly dining. Several of the restaurants offer a vegan menu.

Amusement Parks

A favorite holiday past time are the amusement parks. Each and every summer, amusement parks across the globe are bustling with lots of visitors and long waiting lines. During the course of an adrenaline-filled, muggy day, thrill-seekers become hungry. Unfortunately, these popular, tourist attractions have not yet catered to the vegan community too often.

Most amusement parks offer fast food such as burgers or pizzas. The Six Flags locations across the United States are said to differ slightly from each other, in regard to food options. However, they typically do not offer vegan food. In addition, it is said that visitors are not permitted to bring their own food or snacks into the park. This poses quite a dilemma for vegans.

The other popular, American amusement park system "Disney" has improved over the years and now offers vegan meal options in its locations. Several restaurants at Disney World and Disneyland are vegan-friendly. It is reflected in their menus.

As for small town amusement parks, most likely they are not vegan-friendly. If permitted, it would be best to bring your own vegan food and snacks into the park. It is always worth asking the park's cafes upon arrival. Visitors need to be careful and verify that items like french fries are not cooked in the same oils as the chicken wings. As long as they use separate fryers to cook, the vegan options should be fine.

Vegan Mini-Mall – Portland, Oregon

There is actually a mall located in Portland, Oregon which sells only vegan items. For those who wish to travel there on vacation or for business, you may want to stop at this vegan paradise! It is a mini-mall for vegan businesses. It is located at the northeast corner of Southeast 12th Avenue and Stark Street. There are several vendors selling their vegan-friendly goods in their shops. The vegan businesses located in this mini mall include Herbivore Clothing Company, Sweet Pea Baking Company, Food Fight Grocery, and Scapegoat Tattoo. The like-minded business owners decided to get together to sell products that do not derive from animal sources.

Herbivore Clothing Company –
www.herbivoreclothing.com
This retail outlet sells t shirts, accessories, water bottle holders, belts, handbags, wallets and other items made of non-animal, origin materials. They also sell vegan cookbooks, crafts books, and animal topic books.

Sweet Pea Bakery –
www.sweetpeabakery.com
In addition to typical bakery items such as vegan cakes, brownies, and cupcakes, they sell vegan sandwiches and soups.

Food Fight Grocery –
www.foodfightgrocery.com
Food Fight is a vegan grocery. It seems to be more like a convenience store than a full-fledged grocery store. They sell candy, salty goods such as chips, beverages, fake meats, and some produce. You can also find a selection of baked goods, faux cheese items, savory snacks, international snacks, healthy snacks, condiments, and vitamins.

Scapegoat Tattoo –
www.scapegoattattoo.com
This is a vegan tattoo shop. What that means is that the ink used in the tattoos does not derive from animal origins.

Check out this vegan mini mall on your next stop in Portland!

International Vegan Communities

Did you know that there are actually vegans living together in organized communities across the globe? When you go on holiday, you may want to locate one of these residential groups and may even want to make a decision about residing there yourself. These vegan communities can be found in the mainland USA, Hawaii, and all across Europe, among other places. See libaware.economads.com/veganco.php/. While a couple of them appear to be no longer in business, the other communities have online links which will take you to the home pages of these international community sites.

Residences/Living Space:
These communities do not all have the same goals or living arrangements. You should look at each and determine which is best for you. Some of these communities provide homes for which you can purchase a share and then you may give up your ownership portion when you no longer reside there. Many of these communities offer guest houses for visitors who wish to experience the culture on a temporary basis. The guests are then free to roam around the grounds to check out the property and community. One community allows members to build environmentally friendly homes themselves.

The Food:
While many of the communities appear to be strictly vegan, others are also open to different food options. The main goal is to dine on healthy, organic, eco-friendly, easily sustainable food sources. Some communities produce the organic fruits and vegetables on their own farms. Others purchase healthy, organic produce from nearby farms or markets.

The Lifestyle/Community Goals:
The lifestyle is one of community building and projects with other people who are interested in the environment and healthy eating. Some communities contain an eco-village where everything is environmentally friendly. The homes may be solar powered.

The community may have a shared kitchen which provides community meals. Residents provide funds to contribute to the meals. Community meetings are held to share information on the community and its ecological projects. Classes may be offered which focus on the environment, sustainability, community farming, and permaculture. The goal of these communities is for its members to work together towards sustainability and to build an environmentally safe, eco-friendly world.

Vegan Ethical Issues During World Travels

I'd like to discuss the topic of ethics during travel. I do not have all the answers to these concerns. I would just like to mention them so that you may ponder these issues and come up with your own response. You should be aware of these moral dilemmas.

As a vegan, you may come across some situations during your vacation that challenge your ethics. For example, in certain parts of the world they do not understand veganism at all. Many countries, especially in Africa and Asia feel that a guest is insulting the host by not accepting food that is offered. They do not feel that the host is being rude by not accepting the guest's value system regarding animals. They do not even consider or realize that some people may be vegan due to food allergies, health concerns, or love of animals and non-cruelty. You should determine what your response will be to get out of this sticky situation!

Another concern comes into play whenever a vegan is part of large tour group. The tour guide may have an itinerary that includes activities not suitable for vegans. What do you do? Do you stay at your hotel and opt not to join the group (even if it is included in your tour cost)? Do you attend the activity but not participate?

Animal Rides:
If your tour group goes on a camel ride in Morocco or Egypt, do you not ride yourself because you feel that animals should not be used for our entertainment or carry weight on their back? In Thailand, do you not go on an elephant ride for those same reasons or do you feel that the large animal does not feel any pain from people sitting on its back?

Animals on Display:

In Argentina, Chile, Australia, and New Zealand, would you attend a sheep-shearing event? Do you deem it non-threatening to your vegan morals because the animals do not suffer and it is actually a necessary activity? Would you attend the event to experience the culture?

Shopping at Bazaars or Markets:
Many countries have large, outdoor markets or bazaars which sell everything under the sun. In Mexico and Argentina, they sell lots of leather goods which are displayed prominently throughout these large markets. Would you avoid a market which displays lots of hirachis (leather shoes/sandals) in Mexico or a shop in Argentina that sells many leather crafts? If those markets sell other goods, would you purchase other items there?

Zoos:
Would you visit a zoo in a foreign land if that was your only opportunity to see particular cute and fuzzy animals for which the region is known ? Do you instead refuse to visit zoos because of a moral issue

that animals should not be kept in confinement? In Beijing, China there is a panda bear center where the animals are not confined in cages. They have spacious, grassy areas to graze. Is that satisfactory for a vegan traveler? In Australia, there are animal centers for koalas. Would you consider it unethical to visit or do you prefer to see them in the wild, inside of the rainforest?

Safaris:
Part of the "experience" in an African vacation is to go on safari. In South Africa, there are some reserves and parks where animals were brought to be saved and grow their population. They are not killed by human beings for the consumption of meat. Would a vegan feel comfortable driving around in a safari vehicle just to watch these beautiful animals in motion, not to be killed by humans or predatory animals?

Vegan Clothing, Accessories, and Skincare Products for Your Trip

You should purchase some vegan clothing items and skincare products for your vacation. There are several online clothing stores which sell vegan clothing, jackets, vegan shoes, hiking boots, and rain boots. They also sell vegan accessories such as vegan handbags, backpacks, belts and wallets. The shoes and accessories, of course are not made of leather. The clothing is not made of silk.

Travelers going to the rainforest, for example, would need a pair of hiking boots. Those embarking on lengthy sightseeing tours may need to purchase a pair of sneakers or comfortable, walking shoes. Slippers are a great item to take along on a trip for those cool nights at the hostel or inn. Backpacks would also come in handy for a hike or walking tour. For folks traveling during the rainy season, a pair of rain boots would make a great purchase. Handbags, wallets, and belts are also must-have accessories for any traveler.

Now that you are properly dressed in your vegan attire, you may need some vegan skincare, body care, and cosmetics products for your trip. There are online stores which carry these items also.

You can purchase vegan soaps, facial moisturizers, shower gels, shampoos, hair conditioners, deodorants, toothpastes, base makeup, eyeshadows, and lipsticks. Vegans appreciate the fact that these products not only do not contain animal ingredients such as beeswax or honey, but also they were tested in a cruelty-free environment.

You are now ready to travel in vegan style and comfort, cleaned and ready to conquer the world with a healthy glow on your skin!

The following are shops and online stores which carry vegan clothing, shoes, accessories, skincare, and cosmetics:

Vegan Clothing and Accessories:

Cosmos – clothing, shoes, accessories, skincare:

www.cosmosveganshoppe.com

Alternative Outfitters – shoes, accessories, bags, outerwear:

www.alternativeoutfitters.com/VeganShoes.html

Pangea Vegan Store – clothing, shoes, accessories, skincare:

www.veganstore.com

Cow Jones Industrials – clothing, handbags, shoes

www.cowjonesindustrials.com

Vegan Shoes:

Moo Shoes – shoes (retail and online)

www.mooshoes.com

Sudo Shoes – shoes, slippers, hiking boots, rain boots, handbags, backpacks, wallets, belts (retail and online)

www.sudoshoes.com

Vegan Chic – Vegan shoes

http://www.veganchic.com/

Ragazzi Vegan – Dress and Casual Shoes for men and women

http://www.ragazzivegan.com/

Ethical Wares – Hiking Boots

http://www.ethicalwares.com/

Kerin – Vegan Clothing and Shoes

http://www.kerin.com/

Splaff Flops – Vegan sandals

https://sites.google.com/site/splaffretailsite/

Vegan Coats:

Vaute Couture -

http://www.vautecouture.com/

Vegan Handbags:

Susan Nichole Handbags -

http://susannichole.com/

Crystalyn Kae –

www.crystalynkae.com/vegan-handbags-page-12

Vegan Connection – All-inclusive site which sells clothing, shoes, accessories, skincare:

www.veganconnection.com/where.htm

Vegetarian Channel - Vegetarian Store site lists many vegan manufacturers. They sell clothing, shoes, accessories, skincare.

www.thevegetarianchannel.com/directory/Shopping/Vegetarian_Clothing

Vegan Skincare:

Herbal Choice Mari – Online store selling vegan travel "mini-size" products including shampoos, hair conditioner, toothpaste, shower gel, soap, facial moisturizers. Perfect for travels!

http://www.herbalchoicemari.com

Choice All Natural – vegan skincare products

http://store.skinallnatural.com/skin-all-natural-c2.aspx

Crazy Rumors – vegan lip balm

http://crazyrumors.com/

Lush Cosmetics – vegan hand cream

http://www.lushusa.com/shop/products/body/hand-and-body-creams/handy-gurugu

Rare Natural – vegan skincare products

http://www.rarenatural.com/

Eco Savi Skincare – vegan skincare products

http://www.ecosevi.com/

Alba Botanicals Skincare (some are vegan) –

http://www.albabotanica.com/

Pacifica – vegan skincare products and perfumes

http://www.pacificaperfume.com/

Urban Decay Cosmetics – vegan cosmetics

http://www.urbandecay.com/vegan-cosmetics/9,default,sc.html

Aubrey Organics – vegan skincare products

http://www.pacificaperfume.com/

Vegan, Insect Repellents:

1. Buzz Away" from Quantum Health - This deet-free, chemical-free, insect repellent works well to deter mosquitoes, flies, ticks, gnats.

www.quantumhealth.com/productgroups/itchandbite.html

They manufacture a variety of vegan, bug repellent products including spray bottles, towelettes, candles, and oils.

2. "Bug Ease" by Wise Way Herbals - This product is made with herbs and essential oils. It is also not toxic. It repels both mosquitoes and flies.

Www.wiseways.com

3. "Bite Me Not Spray" sold online by Etsy shop - This repellent is made with essential oils. It repels insects and mosquitoes. It can be sprayed on the body but not the face.

www.etsy.com

4. "Incognito" bug spray by Less Mosquito - This non-toxic spray protects against malaria, mosquitoes, ticks, sandflies, wasps, fleas, bees, midges, and gnats.

www.lessmosquito.com

5. "SunSwat" by Kiss My Face - This vegan product repels bugs and mosquitoes.
www.kissmyface.com/sunpages/sunspraypage.html

6. "Heart Broken Mosquitoes" sold online through Etsy shop - This vegan line offers many options for their insect repellent product, including sprays and bottles.

www.etsy.com

Vegan Luggage and Travel Accessories

While many travel accessories and luggage are made of leather, there are lots of other options. You can find quite a few vendors that manufacture canvas or "faux" leather travel gear. I have found several companies that make vegan luggage, tote bags, passport holders, carry-ons, and so forth.

You can purchase these travel gear items online or in retail stores. Some of the online sites that carry vegan travel gear are the following:

Tom Binh – www.tombihn.com
luggage, tote bags

Broad Bay Cotton – www.broadbaycotton.com
Luggage tags, tote bags, backpacks

Cedar Key Canvas – www.ckcanvas.com
tote bags, luggage, duffle bags

Irvs Luggage - Carries an eco-friendly suitcase and carry-on

www.irvsluggage.com

Ebags - Carries a huge selection of canvas luggage, tote bags, carry-ons, wallets, cosmetics bags, travel blankets, and much, much more!

www.ebags.com/travel_accessories

www.ebags.com/luggage/department

Patagonia, Samsonite, and Land's End carry some vegan, vinyl and canvas luggage also.

Vegan Coupons

Several websites are offering coupons for discounts on vegan products. Anyone can join these sites for free. Membership may include getting added to an email list. These coupon sites provide daily or weekly discounts for a wide variety of vegan products. Members can find bargains on vegan food, snacks, skincare, vegan shoes, and clothing items suitable to maintain a healthy and vegan lifestyle while on vacation. The coupons can be used at local venues, not just for online purchases. This makes it convenient for vegans to shop at discount prices for items they wish to pack for an upcoming holiday excursion!

Discount, vegan coupons are found at:

1. Vegan Coupons(USA website) - http://www.facebook.com/vegancoupons

2. RetailMeNot- http://www.retailmenot.com/coupons/vegan

3. Vegan Cuts(Canadian website) - http://vegancuts.com

International Breads

As you travel throughout the world, you will find many different kinds of breads. Some will be vegan. Some will not. Certain breads contain dairy, honey, or eggs. Of course, if you are dining at a vegan restaurant, there is no need to worry. There are several cultures which usually do not include bread as part of their meals. It is not popular in quite a few South American and Asian countries. However, where it is available during your world travels, I suggest you try the popular, ethnic breads with your meals. Now let us discuss several of these international breads.

France:
Baguette – This is a long, narrow loaf bread with a crispy crust. The bread ingredients are vegan. However, it is typically brushed with an egg yolk mixture on top. Vegans need to ask the chef if this is the case. Otherwise, assume this is the case.

Italy:
Italian Bread – This is also a crusty loaf bread, but it is thick in width.
Again, the ingredients are vegan. However, it is brushed with an egg mixture prior to baking. Vegans should ask the chef if the egg mixture can be omitted.

Greece:
Greek Bread (Horiatiko crusty country bread) – This is a crusty bread typically made containing milk and honey.

Ireland:
Irish Soda Bread – This round, raisin-filled bread contains butter, buttermilk, and eggs. It is not vegan.

Poland:
Babka – This round, Easter bread contains milk and eggs.
A chocolate version is popular.

Portugal:
Portuguese Sweet Bread – This sweet bread is made with milk, honey, and sometimes eggs. It is not vegan.

Portuguese Peasant Bread – This soft, dense, loaf bread is vegan.

Mexico:
Tortillas – This is a round, flatbread made from wheat or corn.
It may either be made with vegetable oil or lard.
Vegan travelers to Mexico should ask their waiter which shortening is used there. It is served with rice and beans or filled with a vegetable mixture as a sandwich.

Israel:
Challah – This is a braided bread served on holidays or the sabbath. It contains eggs, thus is not vegan.

China:
Buns – Steamed buns are popular for dim sum. They are made with yeast and flour. Some are vegan.

Tibet:
Tingmo – These are spongy, steamed buns. They are vegan.

India:
Naan – This is an oven-baked flatbread. It is typically made with ghee(clarified butter) and yogurt. Vegans should ask the restaurant if their version can be made vegan.

Chapati – This is a flatbread served with curry dishes. It is made with vegetable oil and water. Some recipes do call for milk and butter instead. Vegans should ask the waiter in their restaurant of choice.

Parantha – This is also a flatbread made with milled, whole wheat flour. Various recipes call for either ghee or vegetable oil. Again, vegans need to ask the waiter at their dining establishment which shortening the chef uses there.

Mideast (Morocco/Egypt):
Pita Bread – This is a thin, flatbread eaten with hummus, tabbouleh, baba ghanoush, and various other condiments. Made with simple ingredients such as yeast and flour, it is vegan.

Ethiopia:
Injera – This large, round, thin, spongy bread is used for stews to be placed upon it. Pieces of injera are used to scoop up the stew. It is made of Ethiopian teff flour and is vegan.

Nepal/India/Trinidad and Tobago:
Roti – Roti is an Indian puffy bread used to make Doubles sandwiches with a chickpea filling. It is made with yeast, flour, cumin, and curry and is vegan.

International Sauces

As you travel throughout the world, you will find many ethnic dishes that are served with a sauce. While the vegetable, grain, or pasta entree may be vegan itself, the sauce is not necessarily so. Of course, if you are dining in a vegan restaurant, the sauce indeed will be vegan. There are many countries which are known for their distinctive, wonderfully, flavorful sauces. The following will note some of the most popular ethnic sauces, as well as stating whether or not they are vegan.

North America:
Chocolate Mole Sauce – Mexico. This sauce contains Mexican chocolate, chiles, cumin, tomatoes, cumin, and coriander. It is great with tamales or enchiladas. It is vegan, as long as the chocolate does not contain dairy.

Salsa Sauce – Mexico. This sauce contains peppers and tomatoes. It is good with tortillas. It is vegan.

Chili Sauce – Mexico. This sauce contains chiles and tomatoes. It is vegan if the broth is vegetable based. It may be served with tofu or vegetables.

Jamaican Jerk Marinade Sauce – Jamaica. This sauce contains garlic, spices, and peppers. It is vegan. The marinade is typically served with meat. However, if it is served with grilled tofu, it is indeed vegan.

Europe:

Pesto Sauce – Italy. This sauce contains tomatoes, garlic, peppers, and olive oil. Great with pasta. It may or may not be vegan, depending on whether or not it contains cheese. Please ask your waiter.

Al Fredo Sauce – Italy . This sauce contains dairy (cream and butter). It is NOT vegan.

Greek Yogurt Sauce – Greece. This sauce contains dairy (yogurt). It is NOT vegan.

Hollandaise Sauce – France. This sauce contains eggs and butter. It is NOT vegan.

Bernaise Sauce – France. This sauce contains egg yolks and butter. It is NOT vegan.

Roux – France. This sauce contains flour and a fat which is usually butter. It is NOT vegan.

Africa:

Berbere Sauce – Ethiopia. This sauce contains chiles, cumin, allspice, nutmeg, ginger, and cayenne pepper. It is vegan. A great vegan entree would be vegetable stew served with berbere sauce and injera bread.

Harissa Sauce – Morocco/Algeria/Tunisia. This sauce contains chiles, tomatoes, and paprika. It is vegan. Diners will find it being served with pita bread, vegetable entrees, or couscous.

Asia:

Peanut Sauce – Thailand. This sauce may or may not contain fish sauce. As it typically does, it is NOT vegan. Please check with your waiter. Vegan versions may be served with rice and vegetable curry, salads, or pad thai.

Indian Curry – India. This sauce contains ginger, garlic, tomatoes, tumeric. It typically is vegan. Vegetable dishes are served with curry.

Raita Sauce – India. This sauce contains dairy (yogurt). It is NOT vegan.

Thai Curry(Red, Green, Panang, Masaman) – Thailand. This sauce contains chile peppers, coconut milk, and other herbs. It may or may not be vegan. Some restaurants pre-make the sauce with fish sauce. Other restaurants make it as needed and can alter the ingredients to cater to your request for no fish sauce. Every Thai curry is great with tofu and vegetable entrees.

Vegan International Desserts

Finding a good vegan dessert during your global journeys can be extremely difficult. Lets face it..Most desserts are prepared with dairy and/or eggs everywhere in the world. Fortunately, that is not the case in southeast Asian countries. There you can find quite a few vegan-friendly desserts!

The following are a few examples of vegan ethnic desserts:

Maple syrup taffy – You can find this candy in Canada.

Bananas Ghana – bananas with cinnamon, orange juice. You can find this in Ghana.

Bubur cha-cha – sweet potato and yam cubes cooked in coconut milk. This is a Malaysian dessert.

Pulut hitam – black glutinous rice with sago, longan, gula melaka and pandan leaves. This is a Malaysian dessert.

Dreysil – sweet saffron rice with nuts and raisins. This can be found in Tibet.

Mango sticky rice – You can find this sweet dessert in Thailand.

Pumpkin in coconut milk – You can find this dessert in Thailand.

Grass jelly – This treat is made from the mint plant when it is boiled down to a jellylike substance. It may be served with fruit or beans. It is served sometimes in a glass over ice. You may find this dessert in China/Vietnam/southeast Asia.

Mochi rice cakes – These small, round, gooey cakes can be made with sesame, red beans, or green tea. You may find this dessert in Japan.

Che – This is a sweet soup made with tapioca, sweet rice, sweet corn, kidney beans, and coconut milk. This dessert may be found in Vietnam.

Bananas in coconut cream – This dessert is popular in Vietnam.

Chilled longan, lychee, and rambutan fruits – Served over ice. This is popular all over Southeast Asia.

Red beans with syrup and coconut milk – Served in a glass over ice. This is popular in southeast Asia.

Beans (red and kidney), coconut rice, coconut milk, mango, jellies, green tea, tapioca, and exotic fruit(lychee, rambutan, longan)

International Beverages

This travel tip will be regarding popular beverages that you may find in various countries. I, myself am a tea drinker and a consumer of fruit juices. I enjoy green, white, and all kinds of herbal teas. I enjoy many exotic fruit juices such as mango, passionfruit, tamarind, acai, goji berry..and yes, the Durian! The list is too large to mention! There are many varieties of teas and juices which I have found during my world travels. Some of my favorites are acai, goji berry, aloe ferox, and durian juices plus rose mosqueta, hibiscus, and yerba mate teas. These are all vegan, of course!

The following is a list of some beverages (juices and teas) popular in the mentioned countries:

durian juice – Cambodia, Thailand, Malaysia, southeast Asia

acai juice – Brazil

goji juice – China, Himalayas

rose moqueta tea – Argentina

yerba mate tea – Argentina, Chile, Uraguay

hibiscus tea – Egypt

aloe ferox juice – South Africa

Mexican hot chocolate – Mexico
sugar cane juice – Costa Rica

seaweed shake – Belize. For this one, check if they have soymilk version.

guanabana shake – Guatemala. Again, ask for soymilk version.

chicha con arroz y piña - Panama. rice and boiled pineapple beverage.

chicha de marañón – Panama. beverage made from fruit of cashew tree.

Chicha Morada juice – Peru. Purple corn with sugar

sorrel juice – Jamaica

mint tea – Israel

Turkish tea – Turkey

kiwi juice – New Zealand

International Spice Markets

Several countries around the globe are known for their bazaars, souks, or markets where they sell their aromatic herbs and spices.

When I visited Egypt, my tour group was fortunate enough to be invited to a local spice shop by our guide. She frequented this market hidden in a winding alleyway. The locals love it. Although the Aswan and Cairo markets are known for spices also, this one was located in Luxor, in central Egypt.

.
This region is known for its wide variety of spices. They actually carry herbs and spices from all over Africa. The ones I purchased derived from places such as Morocco, South Africa, Egypt, and other African destinations. In total, I bought around fifteen or so spices and herbs. They included cumin, coriander, mint, parsley, basil, tumeric, curry, oregano, saffron, black/green/red pepper, vanilla, ginger, nutmeg, cloves, and cinnamon! The scents were very captivating! offer a A free bag of hibiscus leaves for brewing tea was my free gift for making a large purchase.

Spice shops typically display their goods in large, round baskets in their storefront. The vendors will scoop up as much a quantity as you wish to purchase. The fresh, local versions of spices and herbs taste so different and so much richer than their supermarket chain counterparts. The taste is much stronger and flavorful!

Other destinations known for great spice markets are the bazaars of Turkey, Morocco, Thailand and India. The Asian markets carry spices such as galanga, lemongrass, Indian curry, and cardamon. These spices are used in Thai and Indian cuisines such as curries, pad Thai, Italian, and stir-fries.

Spices can be found in the Floating Markets of Thailand. In places such as mainland China or Hong Kong, you can find shops which sell more medicinal herbs. You can find herbal remedies for a wide variety of ailments such as headaches, stomach aches, aging, and stress.

Several of these remedies derive from the plant and tree sources. They are typically brewed in a tea, not consumed in prepared foods. The prices of herbs and spices vary depending on their rarity and desirability. Edible herbs and spices are affordable and can be purchased at minimal cost. The medicinal herbs, however can be very expensive. Some can be purchased for just a few dollars, while others can run up to thousands of dollars.

Vegan Options at Highway Rest Area Stops

During your road trips, you will undoubtedly make a stop for lunch, dinner, or a snack. You may experience your hunger pangs while on route by car. You may even be on the highway where the closest opportunity for a meal may be the rest area stop. These have presented problems for vegans for ions!

Rest areas can present some of the most frustrating experiences for vegan travelers! Vegans are lucky if they can find a fast food restaurant there that even provides a salad without cheese. The best option if you are unsure of the destination is to bring your own trail mix, crackers, vegan sandwiches such as tofurkey, or to bring dry packaged noodles or Indian meals that just need hot water.

United States:
The rest area "food court" typically includes such non-vegan-friendly, fast food restaurants as McDonald's, Burger King, Pizza Hut, and Starbucks.
I recently came across a wonderful vegan dining experience at a rest area stop in Massachusetts off the Mass. Turnpike! This particular rest stop included a Fresh City cafe. They had a few options on their menu with a "V" next to it. I chose a delicious Asian veggie wrap which was vegan.

I have never rented an auto in another country. However, travelers who do rent cars also need to be concerned about vegan options at rest area stops in other countries.

United Kingdom/Great Britain:
In the UK, highway rest areas are referred to as "motorway service stations".

Marks and Spencer Simply Food stores are located at many rest stops in England, Scotland, and the rest of Great Britain.

These stores sell vegan sandwiches. It is difficult to find vegan fare at the motorway service stations in the UK, so this store is a welcomed find!

Europe:
Each European country varies in the quantity and quality of rest area dining.

Veganism is still uncommon in France. Auto-routes in France have some full service facilities. However, do not expect anything vegan to eat at rest stops in the country.

In Germany, it is also difficult to find any vegan fare along the roadways.

There is a restaurant in Austria called Landzeit. They have locations along the autobahn. Their huge salads are a great choice for vegans.

Australia:
Australia rest areas do not include restaurants. They may have a caravan serving beverages and snacks for the weary traveler. There are other facilities called

roadhouses for travelers which contain restaurants. The roadhouses typically do not have vegan meal options. It is recommended to bring your own food while on a road trip here.

Asia:
Rest areas in Asia do have restaurants on site. Malaysian highways have restaurant facilities located above the expressway. In Thailand, rest stops usually include curry or noodle restaurants. These are good possibilities for vegans, but be prepared to ask if the dishes contain fish sauce.

My Vegan "Best Of"

I would like to share the names and locations of my vegan "Best Of" in the United States including a wonderful bakery, ice cream shop, donut shop, breakfast cafe, and dim sum restaurant. As you travel to different parts of the country, be sure to sample the delicious vegan selections from the following places!

1. Best Vegan Dim Sum – Vegetarian Dim Sum House – Chinatown, New York City.
www.yelp.com/biz/vegetarian-dim-sum-house-new-york
The huge variety of items here is incredible. You may choose from steamed buns, scallion pancakes, pastries wonton soup, lotus root cakes, red bean cake, crispy banana rolls, turnip cakes, corn congee, and much more.

2. Best Vegan Bakery – Sticky Fingers – Washington, DC.
www.stickyfingersbakery.com
Cakes, cupcakes(unique flavors), pies, cookies, cinnamon buns, muffins, breads, and more.

3. Best Vegan Ice Cream – Lula's Sweet Apothacary – New York, NY
http://www.lulassweetapothecary.com/
Many different flavors, including unique flavors, sundaes, and banana splits.

4. Best Vegan Breakfast/Brunch – The Chicago Diner – Chicago and Spiral Diner – Dallas
www.veggiediner.com/wp/
www.spiraldiner.com
Vegan burritos, tofu scramble, faux sausage, biscuits and gravy, smoothies and much more.

5. Best Vegan Donuts – MightYo – Seattle, WA www.mightyo.com Many decadent flavors with various toppings and icings, such as chocolate raspberry, cinnamon and sugar, french toast, and lemon poppy.

6. Best Vegan Brunch Buffet – Indigo Cafe – Concord, NH www.cafeindigo.com

Worldwide Vegetarian/Vegan Festivals

Boston Vegetarian Food Festival
Reggie Lewis Athletic Center
1350 Tremont Street, Boston, Massachusetts

Viva! Incredible Veggie Roadshow
Bath, England

Brighton Eco Veggie
Fayre, England

Northumberland, England
www.ecoveggiefayre.co.uk

Pennsylvania, USA
North American Vegetarian Summerfest

World Congress
different global location every year

Phuket Vegetarian Festival
Phuket, Thailand

Vegan Festival
Adelaide, Australia

Vegetarian Food Fair
Toronto, Canada

VegFest
Seattle, WA

VeggieFest Chicago
Chicago, IL

Vegan Camp
Snettisham, Hunstanton, Scotland

My Restaurant Recommendations

The following are vegan or veggie-friendly restaurants where I've enjoyed dining during my global travels!

Canada:

"Bo De Duyen", Address: 1999 Dundas Street,Toronto

"Aux Vivres", 4631 boul. St-Laurent, Montreal

"Bonnys", 1748 Rue Notre-Dame Ouest, Montreal

"Crudessence", 105 Rachel W Street, Montreal

Mexico:

Vegetariano Zanahoria, Address: Avenida Americas 332, Guadalajara

Trinidad:

Mother Nature, Address: Abercromby & Park St, Port Of Spain

Brazil:

Vegetariano Social Clube Culinaria Organica ,
Address: Conde de Bernadote 26, loja L (at
Leblon)Rio

Chile:

El Huerto, www.elhuerto.cl/index, Address: Orrego
Luco, 54, Santiago

Govindas, www.govinda.cl/spanish/inicio.html,
Address: Santa Rosa 218, Puerto Varas

Argentina:

Pura Vida Restaurant, Address: Av. del Libertador
1876, El Calafate

Peru:

Café Lashesh (Vegan options the BEST felafel ever!),
Address: Av. Diagonal 358Lima, Miraflores, Lima

Govindas (traditional Peruvian cuisine at this
location), Address:Espaderos 128 (084), Cusco

Iceland:

A Naestu Grosum, http://www.anaestugrosum.is/,
Address: Laugavegur 20b

Singapore:

Food Republic (one of many food courts/hawker stalls), Address: 1 HarbourFront Walk

South Africa:

Lolas, Address: 228 Long Street, Capetown

Rootis (Cape Malay cuisine), Address: Shop 1 Piazza Level Clock Tower Centre,V&A Waterfront,Capetown

Addis In Cape (Ethiopian Vegan options), Address: 41 Church St (at Long St), Capetown

Mama Afrika (Vegan options), mamaafricarest.net/, Address: 178 Long Street, Capetown

Africa Café (Vegan options), africacafe.co.za/, Address: 108 Shortmarket Street, Capetown

Vegan Top World Restaurants:
World's Top 50 Vegan/Vegetarian Restaurants: From 2007. However, it gives the traveler a good idea of dining choices.
www.airlinecreditcards.com/travelhacker/top-50-vegan-and-vegetarian-restaurants-in-the-world

Healthy Souvenir Products

Whenever I travel, I look for souvenirs or vegan foods that are indigenous to that destination. It especially interests me if that particular ingredient, plant, or food derives only from that region. When I find those items, they are what I eat at the local restaurants or purchase as souvenirs.

The following are indigenous, region-specific, vegan products I have found during my travels:

1. **South Africa -**

   Aloe Ferox ointments, moisturizing creams, teas, juices. The Aloe Ferox plant has healing properties that have the reputation of healing burns & scars and moisturizing skin.
   Rooibos Tea – anti-oxidant properties. I purchased Rooibos tea and also skin cream.

2. **Argentina** – Rose Mosqueta moisturizing creams and tea. Great for skin.

3. **Egypt** – Plentiful spice markets are found here. Buy herbs & spices from all over Africa. The popular local ones are cumin, cardamon, mint, oregano, basil, curry, ginger, vanilla, saffron, hibiscus(for making tea), various ground peppers, cinnamon, and nutmeg.

4. **Brazil** – Acai berry only grows here. The highest anti-oxidant levels we can consume. Extremely healthy! Purchase acai foods, beverages, teas, and skincare products such as moisturizing creams.

5. **China** – The amount and varieties of medicinal teas here are phenomenal! You can purchase teas for stomach aches, memory, sleep deprivation, anti-aging, everything that ails you physically and emotionally! I recommend purchasing some of these.

6. **Greece** – Any product containing olives, moisturizers, etc. Very good for skin. The South African "wine country" region is also known for growing olives. I purchased some wonderful olive hand cream there in shop dedicated to olive-based products. Don't forget to snack on them too!

Section 2:

This section provides information on the dining scene in each continent. Popular breakfast foods, lunch options, and dinners are discussed for many of the frequently visited countries across the globe.

Local fruits, beverages, and desserts are discussed. The vegan alternatives in meat-centric countries are suggested. Finally, the availability of vegan-friendly restaurants in each country is reviewed.

North America

United States

The United States does not have a particular national dish. There are regions of the USA which are recognized for their own cuisine. For example, southern cuisine is influenced by the African farmers who were brought there. Creole and Cajun peoples have influenced southern Louisiana cooking. Soul food hails from the south also. Native Americans also added to the cuisine of every region of the country. Coastal areas such as New England produce their own cuisine.

The great news here in the United States is that great vegan food is available in many major cities and growing in popularity. Quite a few states claim vegetarian or vegan organizations. More and more vegan restaurants are opening across the country. America is slowly becoming veganized!

Restaurants:

There are many vegan and vegan-friendly restaurants in the northeastern part of the United States and in the west. The Midwest and the South are not as vegan-friendly. However, herbivores may be able to find some suitable restaurants.

Canada

Quebec's popular dish is Poutine. It is French fries covered in gravy. Pancakes with maple syrup may also be considered a national dish.

Breakfast:

Popular breakfasts in Canada are similar to breakfasts in the USA. It typically consists of croissants, cereal, toast, waffles, or pancakes (with maple syrup), along with coffee, tea, or orange juice.

For lunch and dinner, Canadians consume a lot of fish and pork. Soups such as French Pea Soup and sandwiches are popular at lunch time also. Every region boasts of their own specialties. However, there are some traditional cuisines in each region which have a few veggie-friendly options such as potato balls (vegan version- no ham or cheese) and yellow pea soup(vegan version). Check for these at the local vegan restaurants. The original recipes are not vegan. Try to locate a vegan restaurant which serves poutine fries without a meat-based gravy. British Columbia is recognized for its vegan dining!

Beverages:

The beverages consumed in Canada are similar to the USA – soft drink, juices, coffee, and tea.

Restaurants:

The Montreal region is vegan-friendly. Quebec has one or two vegan-friendly restaurants, as does Halifax, Nova Scotia. Vancouver, British Columbia is extremely vegan-friendly with quite a few vegan dining establishments. Toronto is very vegan-friendly also with the Chinatown district containing many vegan restaurants.

Mexico

Staples of Mexican food include beans and corn. Squash and peppers play an important role in the cuisine also. Spices such as chile powder, cumin, oregano, cocoa, and cinnamon are popular. Rice is also an important staple in Mexican cuisine.

Each region of Mexico produces different kinds of cuisine. Northern Mexico is known for its meat dishes. Southeastern Mexico is well known for spicy vegetable dishes and chicken. Seafood is popular in some regions. In jungle regions beware of the forest creatures which appear on the menu! The Mexican cuisine was influenced by Mayan, Aztec, and Spanish peoples. Some traditional Mexican staples include tortillas, beans, and chile peppers. The country grows a cornucopia of fruits and vegetables such as tomatoes, corn, sweet potatoes, squash, avocado, coconut, pineapple, papaya, cactus, and prickly pear.

Each meal in Mexico consists of tortilla selections. It is often stuffed with eggs, cheese, or beans. It's a typical staple of breakfast in Mexico. Refried black or pinto beans (frijoles) are typically part of breakfast also. Vegans beware, as they are usually fried in lard. Only order them at vegan restaurants.

Mexicans love chocolate. It is darker and more bitter than European or American chocolate. The Mexicans sometimes mix their chocolate with sugar, cinnamon, or ground chile peppers. It is often mixed with water or milk (ask for soymilk) as a breakfast beverage. Mexican hot chocolate is a thick, sweet dessert.

Breakfast:

Mexicans usually have sweet rolls and coffee or fresh juice in the morning. Tortillas are sometimes a popular breakfast option, as are fresh fruit or refried beans. Vegans should ask if the beans are cooked in lard or animal stock.

Brunch:

Fresh fruit is enjoyed for brunch in large quantities. The selection of fruits includes avocados, bananas, grapes, guavas, mangoes, kiwis, pineapples, and prickly pears.

Snacks:

Botanas are snacks such as salted peanuts or nachos and salsa. Mexicans munch on botanas throughout the day.

Comida:

Comida is the main meal of the day eaten in the mid-afternoon.

It typically includes soup or salad a main dish and a dessert. The main dish may be a tortilla, frijoles, stuffed chile peppers, enchiladas, quesadillas, tacos, mole, or tostadas. Vegan restaurants should have the vegan versions of these entrees without cheese or meats, and not cooked in lard. Usually the beverage of choice is a fruit-flavored water referred to as agua fresca.

Cena:

Many Mexicans may only chose to have a hot drink and some bread for the final meal of the day. Others prefer something a little more substantial such as tacos.

Restaurants:

The touristy Mexican cities (Mexico City, Guadalajara, etc) have some vegan-friendly restaurants. However, vegans need to be careful in villages and remote areas, as wild game and mammals are eaten more commonly than vegetables.

Central America:

Costa Rica:

Breakfast:

Gallo Pinto (rice and beans) is a popular breakfast meal. Agua dulce or sugar cane water is a beverage usually served at breakfast time.

Lunch:

At lunchtime, Casado is typical. This is a rice and beans entrée combined with cabbage and tomato salad, fried plantains, and meat. Look for the vegan version at veggie-friendly restaurants. Fruit juice is a beverage of choice.

Costa Rican staples include beef, chicken, fish, and seafood. Vegetable dishes are not popular here.

Dinner:

Casados are the typical dinner meal also.

Costa Rican appetizers are known as bocas. Tamales (stuffed cornmeal patties wrapped and steamed inside banana leaves), patacones (fried green plantain chips), and fried yucca are veggie appetizers which you may be able to find at vegan-friendly restaurants.

In general, vegetables are not an important part of Costa Rican meals. They may just be little slices included on a dish. A palmito, palm salad is more filling. A side dish such as picadillo, a stew of vegetables is another option. However, ask if it contains a bit of meat in it. Fortunately, there are some vegan-friendly restaurants in the capital of San Jose where veggie options will not be a problem. The countryside is not very vegan-friendly in Costa Rica. Fried plantains are a great vegan option in restaurants. Yucca is another vegetable option in Costa Rica.

Costa Rica grows a vast amount of tropical fruits. Some of these are papayas, pineapples, melons, and bananas. Other fruits include marañón (the fruit of the cashew tree); passion fruit, and carambola (star fruit).

Beverages:

Some popular Costa Rican beverages include Horchata, a cinnamon cornmeal drink, Chan, a drink made with seeds, Linaza, and Fresco de Frutas. The best quality coffee is usually exported.

Fruits:

Mango, passion fruit, guanabana, and tamarind are popular lunch time fruit juice beverages. These are made of fruits diluted in water. Be sure to ask, however, if they are diluted in milk, as is sometimes the case.

Restaurants:

The villages of Costa Rica are not very vegan-friendly. The capital of San Jose has a few vegan-friendly restaurants.

Belize

Belizean cuisine is derived from Carribean, Mexican, Mayan, Spanish and African influences. Pizza, Chinese food, and Indian food are popular here also. Vegans may enjoy dining at an Indian restaurant whenever a vegan dining establishment can not be found. Unfortunately, seafood is a staple here also. Rice and beans is usually served with most meals. Spicy hot sauce is readily found at restaurants.

Breakfast:

For breakfast, Belizeans typically eat scrambled eggs and refried beans. Often, it is accompanied a selection of tortillas, johnnycakes (biscuit with ham or cheese), or fry jacks (biscuit with sugar).

Lunch/Dinner:

Cassava bread or rice and beans are popular side dishes with typical meals. The main entrée is usually ceviche, tamales, or boil ups. Meat, Wild Game, and Seafood are popular in Belize. Vegan dining establishments may have a "faux seafood", vegan version of ceviche. Vegetables are not an important part of Belizean meals. Slaws, salads, or potatoes may be considered a side dish.

Cafes and roadside stalls will serve tacos, tamales, or garnaches (fried, corn tortilla with beans, cheese, or meat). Check for vegan versions of these snacks.

Fruits:

Belize grows a large variety of tropical fruits. Mangoes, papayas, pineapples, melons, and bananas are common. The cashew tree fruit, and carambola (star fruit) grow here also.

Beverages:

Fresh juices and tropical fruit shakes are popular such as mango or papaya. Seaweed shakes are made with milk (check if soymilk available), cinnamon, and nutmeg.

Restaurants:

There are no vegan restaurants in Belize capital.

The only options are Chinese or Indian restaurants or one of the vegan-friendly restaurants in town.

Guatemala

Mayan, Spanish, and Chinese cultures influence the cuisine in Guatemala. Tortillas, rice and black beans are usually part of every meal. Turkey and beef are popular in most regions, while seafood is popular along the coast. For vegans, guacamole, yucca, carrots, and plantains are available. Chile Rellenos (stuffed chiles) and tamales (meat and cornmeal in banana leaves) are very common dishes also.

Breakfast:

The breakfast in Guatemala usually consists of eggs, refried beans, and tortillas. Sometimes fresh fruit, cheese, or plantains will be served as a side. Vegans should verify that the beans are not cooked in lard.

Lunch/Dinner:

Stews, soups, veggie burgers, tamales, chile rellenos (stuffed chiles), and enchiladas are typical meals. Side dishes may include tacos, corn, beans, rice, and cheese. Look for vegan versions of these. Guatemalans eat snacks such as empanadas (stuffed with meat or potatoes), tacos, burritos, or tamales. Look for vegan versions of these.

Vegetables are not popular side dishes or main meal options in Guatemala. Meals may include cabbage slaw or a potato. Vegan restaurants may have some of the commonly grown vegetables in the country such as yucca or plantains.

Fruits:

Guatemala is abundant with tropical fruits. Bananas, mangoes, papayas, pineapples, and watermelons are some of the typical ones found here. The carambola (star fruit) and the guanabana (soursop) are also common.

Beverages:

Common fruit shakes are made with papaya, pineapple, mango, or guanabana. Vegans can order them made in water. Lemonade mixed with fizzy water is very popular.

Restaurants:

In general, Guatemala is not a vegan-friendly country. Guatemala City only has one vegan-friendly restaurant. Vegans need to ask restaurant staff if they would serve common vegetables such as corn or yucca. Also important is to ask whether or nor rice and beans can be made without lard or animal stock.

Panama

Food in Panama is not much different than that in other Latin American countries. However, it is not as spicy. Corn is a popular staple in the food here. Fish and chicken are a big part of Panamanian cuisine. Vegetarians and vegans may delight in a popular food called patacones (fried plantain slices). Although there are local fruits grown here, they are not typically served in restaurants. They may be purchased instead at roadside stands. Indigenous, Spanish, Carribean, and African influences make up the cuisine.

Breakfast:

Breakfast in Panama typically include corn tortillas, eggs and fried meat. Fresh fruit and toast are available for vegans. Hojaldras which are deep-fried bread pieces with sprinkled powdered sugar, similar to doughnuts, are also typical breakfast staples. Vegans should ask in local vegan-friendly cafes, if a vegan version of this donut is available. Coffee is the beverage of choice.

Lunch/Dinner:

A typical meal in Panama includes meat such as a sancocho stew, ceviche, or empanadas, coconut rice and beans. Fruits and vegetables such as yucca, squash, mangoes, pineapple, papaya, passion fruit, soursop, guanabana, and plantains can accompany the meal and are a great option for vegans. Fried yucca rolls and tamales are common side dishes. Vegans should seek these at vegan-friendly dining establishments.

Beverages:

Coconut juice (pipa) and chicha (fruit juice made from local exotic fruits such as cashew tree fruit or naranjilla) are popular beverages in the cities and towns, as well as at roadside stands. Another local beverage is chicheme, which is a corn-based beverage mixed with water, sugar, and cinnamon.

Restaurants:

Panama is not a very vegan-friendly country, as there is only one vegan-friendly restaurant in Panama City and one in David. However, there are several common vegetables prepared at side dishes. Vegans may ask for these at non-vegan restaurants. Chinese restaurants (Or other ethnic restaurants) are the best dining options for vegans traveling away from the capital of Panama City.

There are many ethnic groups represented in Panama. These immigrant groups brought their varied cuisine with them as is obvious in the dining scene. In Panama City, the visitor will find French, Japanese, Italian, Thai, Italian, Middle Eastern, and Chinese restaurants. Outside of Panama City, there are many Chinese restaurants. These would be the best source for vegan dining.

Carribean

Trinidad and Tobago

Vegans will love Trinidad! There are quite a few amazing, local vegetables that are popular here. Calalloo is enjoyed in this country and is even considered a national dish of Trinidad and Tobago. Calallo soup is a thick soup made with the leaves of the dasheen vegetable.

Breakfast:

Although fish and eggs are main breakfast staples, there are vegan options too.

Doubles are a sandwich of roti bread filled with chickpeas (easy to find at road side stands). Other vegan favorites are fried dasheen cakes, boiled cassava, or roasted eggplant. Breads or biscuits are served cold.

Lunch/dinner:

Curry Chicken and Roti or fish are popular for carnivores. However, Bake N Veggies are available for vegans. This Bake N Veggies sandwich is available at Maracas beach. Stall vendors sell these popular lunch time sandwiches. Calallo soup is a great vegan selection. It is often served with cornmeal, plantain, cassava, or sweet potatoes. For fruit selections, there are mangoes, breadfruit, sorrel, passionfruit, sapodillas, pomerac, papaya, apples, oranges, cherries, carambola, soursop, coconuts, watermelons, pineapples, and bananas, among others.

Street foods are good choices for tourists as they make their way along the coast to the beach for the day. Some common street vendor vegan snacks are doubles, corn soup,or potato pies. For something sweet, snow cones are the snack of choice.

Beverages:

Popular beverages include coconut water, sorrel juice, and soursop punch.

Restaurants:

Considering the local vegetable options and the wonderful vegan-friendly restaurant in Port Of Spain, Trinidad appears to be very vegan-friendly! Tobago does not have many choices for vegan dining. However, Kariwak Village serves amazing vegan Indian fare.

Puerto Rico

Puerto Rican cuisine is a blend of Spanish, African, Taíno, and American styles. Coriander, papaya, cacao, nispero, apio, and plantains are common ingredients in their cuisine. Puerto Ricans refer to their cuisine as "cocina criolla"(Creole cooking). This indigenous population lived on corn, fruit, and seafood. The Spanish brought wheat, rice and sugarcane, while the Africans introduced okra and taro to the local diet. Great for vegans! The island cuisine is a combination of ingredients and flavors from each of the ethnic groups here.

Breakfast:

For breakfast, Puerto Ricans typically consume juice, hot chocolate, fruits, plantains and toasted bread. It is an important meal here.

Lunch/Dinner:

Soups and stews are usually part of the lunch and dinner menu in Puerto Rico. They are made with sofrito, which is a coriander, garlic, onion, sweet pepper, oregano and tomato puree, sauteed blend. Black bean soup is a popular dish. Vegans may delight in a soup made with chickpeas. Verify that the broth is of vegetable base, not chicken or beef broth. Also, vegans should ask if there are bones included in the broth. Plantains and yams are an important part of Puerto Rican meals. They may be prepared baked, mashed, sautéed, or fried. Some other popular vegetables and vegan choices are beans, corn, pigeon peas, rice, potatoes, yucca. Plantain tostones are common also.

Mofongo is a dish made with fried plantains or yucca. It is important to only select this entrée in a restaurant that makes it without the use of pork. Fried cornmeal logs, referred to as "sorullos" are a good vegan option, when made without cheese. In non-vegan restaurants, be prepared to ask if the rice dish contains bits of meat.

Fruits:

Visitors will find many delicious, tropical fruits including passionfruit, mango, star fruit, soursop, plantains, tamerind, and mamey sapote, among others.

Restaurants: The capital of San Juan only has one vegan restaurant, but quite a few vegan-friendly restaurants. However, in the villages, people indulge in a meat-based cuisine that may pose some problems for vegans. It requires vegans to ask the standard questions in restaurants such as "Can the meal be prepared without lard or animal-based stock?"

Bahamas

Being an island nation, seafood is a huge part of Bahamian cuisine. Peas and rice are also important staples in the diet. However, vegans must ask for a version that does not contain pork. Vegans can not eat the popular Johnny Cake, because this bread is made with milk and butter.

Restaurants:

No vegan or veggie-friendly restaurants exist in Nassau.

The best bet is for vegans to try the Indian restaurant in town.

Jamaica

Spanish, Indian, East Asian, and English settlers influenced the Jamaican cuisine with a variety of flavors and spices.

Breakfast:

Ackee, a local fruit and fish are popular breakfast food for the locals along with callaloo, boiled green bananas, or Johnny Cake (a sweet bread). A great vegan breakfast may also include cornmeal, plantains or peanut porridge.

Roadside vendors abound in Jamaica. However, they are not the best option for vegans. Fish is a major ingredient incorporated into roadside snacks.

Jamaicans do enjoy their vegetables. Usually, they are included in local beverages such as carrot juice or beetroot juice mixed with Jamaican herbs. Ting is a local citrus drink. Sorrell is a drink that may have healing properties. Coconut water is a common beverage here. Fresh juices such as soursop, tamarind, and guava are good choices too.

Lunch/Dinner:

Curried "Jerk", meat dishes are popular in Jamaica. However, there are options for vegans that include rice and peas, or soups such as bean or pumpkin. Various breads such as bammy or hard bread are served with meals. Yucca and okra are good options too. Fruits such as star apple and breadfruit are eaten as snacks and included in desserts.

Ital food (eye-tal) is Rastafarian food. This is vegetarian cooking style that does not use salt in their dishes. This cuisine consists of vegetables, rice, beans, and herbs and spices.

Beverages:

There are quite a few local fruits that make popular beverages. These include mango, soursop, sorrel, soursop, and tamarind juice. Peanut punch is a common beverage.

Restaurants:

Jamaica is vegan-friendly despite the love of meat there. There are wonderful local vegetable dishes, in addition to vegan restaurant dining options.

Mid East

Israel

Certain meats are part of the Israeli diet. However, pork and shellfish are not considered kosher. There are plentiful vegan options, including some Arab influenced dishes such as felafel.

Chinese, Mexican, Thai, Italian, Italian, and Indian restaurants are commonplace in Israel. Vegans may find good dining here.

Breakfast:

For breakfast, a typical meal would consist of vegetables salad, cheese, bread, olives, and eggs. Vegans, of course may omit the cheese and eggs. Turkish coffee or juice is the beverage of choice.

Lunch/Dinner:

Meals typically start with appetizers. Stuffed vegetables may be part of the meal also. Soups are served next. Lentil soup is a great vegan choice, if it is made without animal stock. A meat or poultry-based main dish follows. Pastries or fruit are served as the dessert. Mint tea is a favored beverage. Salhab is a beverage made from the orchid.

For vegans, some of the Arab cuisine is suitable such as mujadara (rice and lentils), couscous, or hummus in pita bread. Dips such as Baba ghanoush (eggplant) or tabbouleh contain strictly vegan ingredients.

The felafel (pita bread with chickpeas) is a common snack food, as is the boureka, a pastry stuffed with cheese or potato.

Salads play an important part in Israeli meals. Avocado, carrot, or green pepper salads are popular choices. These are great for vegan diners!

Restaurants:

The large cities in Israel such as Jerusalem and Tel Aviv are fairly vegan-friendly.

Jordan

Syria, Lebanon, and Palestine influence the cuisine in Jordan. Meat, chicken and lamb dishes play important roles in the meals. Shish kebabs will please the meat lovers. There are stuffed grape leave dishes which may be vegan. Grains, rice, and vegetables are important food staples so vegans should be happy here.

Breakfast:

The first meal of the day is simple. Jordanians will start each morning with croissants or bread, jam, and tea. Often pastries may be served.

Lunch/Dinner:

Arabic appetizers, called mezze, are a huge part of the cuisine in Jordan. These include hummous and Ful Moudames (fava beans). Sahlab is a popular drink made from the starch in orchid bulbs. Tea and coffee are served with main meals also.

Lunch is the main meal. This consists of meat, poultry, or fish, rice, lentil soup, bread and vegetables, plus a side salad. Couscous, felafel, or fatoush in pita bread make for good vegan fare. Eggplant, zucchini, and olives are vegetables that can be found in Arab cuisine. Popular fruits here are dates, figs, and pomegranates.

Desserts:

Some well-loved desserts in Jordan are rice pudding, maamoul, katayef (similar to baklava), or kanafe (look for vegan version with soya cheese if possible).

Restaurants:

There are no vegan or vegetarian restaurants in Jordan. However, Arabic food such as felafel, hummous, baba ghanoush, fool moudames, and side dishes of vegetables are good vegan options.

Turkey

Arab influenced food is great for vegan diners!

Breakfast:

The first meal of the day usually consists of tomatoes, cheese, black olives, bread with jam, and eggs. Of course, vegans should omit the eggs and cheese. Sourdough bread accompanies the meal. Tea is the beverage of choice.

Lunch:

Various types of soups are a main staple during lunch or dinner. Lentil or vegetable soups are popular. Lamb or chicken is usually served for carnivores grilled or in kebab form. For vegans, eggplant dishes, rice or bulgar pilaf dishes are also popular.

Dinner:

Appetizers are served before dinner. There are several vegetables appetizers from which to choose. The main course consists of soup(ask for no meat stock), pilaf, and vegetables for vegans. Wheat and rice are common ingredients for Turkish cuisine, as are vegetables such as eggplant. Zucchini, artichokes, and cabbage are beloved vegetables in the Turkish food also. Beans are common in the cuisine also. Borek is a pastry filled with meat, cheese, or vegetables.

Yogurt is often served with meat and vegetable dishes. Vegans should ask for the vegetable dish to be prepared without yogurt. While vegetables are plentiful in the typical Turkish meal, one must be careful as small amounts of meat are used in vegetable dishes for flavoring. Be sure to verify this at restaurants and have the meat omitted.

Beverages:

The beverages consumed with meal may be Turkish coffee, Turkish tea, or fruit juice.

Restaurants:

The Turkish dining scene does not have many vegan restaurants. However, vegetables are an important part of Turkish cuisine, so the savvy traveler should ask for vegan fare in restaurants to be prepared without any animal, poultry, or fish products.

Australia

Food in Australia has been influenced by India, China, Japan, Thailand, and Vietnam. Greek, Italian, and Lebanese immigrants had a huge impact on the cuisine also.

Breakfast:

Breakfast is usually cereal, Weet Bix (wheat biscuit), vegemite spread on toast, Tim Tams, or fruit. Beverages consumed in the morning include tea, coffee, or juice.

Lunch/Dinner:

Barbequed meat is extremely popular in Australia. Vegetables are served with most meals. Vegans also have choices such as international cuisine from Asia or Middle East, pasta (no eggs or cheese) or pizza (no cheese). Juices such as passionfruit are a refreshing beverage.

Fruit:

Breadfruit, jabuticaba, black sapote are local exotic fruits from this region.

Restaurants:

The large cities in Australia are very vegan-friendly. Sydney and Melbourne have a great vegan dining scene. There are many vegan restaurants. Many other ethnic cuisines are represented in the dining scene such as Chinese or other restaurants. The Outback region may present problems for vegans.

New Zealand

British, Italian, Asian, Indian, and Maori cultures influence the food.

The local cuisine does consist of a lot of meat dishes such as lamb, mutton, beef, chicken, or seafood. Vegetables abound in city cuisine also. The rural areas may pose a problem for vegans.

Breakfast:

A typical breakfast in New Zealand consists of toast possibly with a vegemite spread, cereal, juice and fruit. Porridge or Weet-Bix is preferred during colder months.

Lunch/Dinner:

Hangi is a traditional Maori dish made of meat and vegetables placed under heated rocks to cook. Vegan-friendly restaurants may possibly have a vegan version consisting only of vegetables.

Vegans may consume such vegetables as eggplants, beetroot, zucchinis, kumara (similar to sweet potato), asparagus, and tamarillos (tree tomatoes). Other options include dining at the vegan-friendly Asian, Indian, or European restaurants in town.

Beverages:

Tropical fruit juices are popular beverages.

Fruit:

bilberries, kiwis, gooseberries, rock melons, loganberries, and passionfruit are local fruits from New Zealand.

Restaurants:

Rural areas could present a problem for vegans. Major cities are quite vegan-friendly with quite a few restaurants. There are also other ethnic restaurants such as Indian or Chinese at which to find vegan dining options.

Antarctica

Antarctica is becoming sought after holiday destination these days. Travelers are interested in visiting the southern tip of the earth. Obviously there are no cities or towns on the continent. However, there are research headquarters there.

The chefs do prepare meals for visitors with special request, whether it is for health concerns or for vegan diets.

Ships:

Anyone travelling by ship to Antarctica must request a vegan meal on board prior to departure and/or bring vegan foods with them. Buffets should have some vegetable options.

There are research facility bases on Antarctica. They have a restaurant or dining quarters in the compound. Food supplies, including vegetables are brought aboard the ships or by plane. Chefs speak to the visitors to determine what kind of ingredients they need and what kind of meals to prepare.

South America

Peru

Many cultures have left an impact on the cuisine of Peru. Spanish, African slaves, Chinese immigrant workers, and Italians play an influential role in the food here. While seafood and chicken is popular in Peru, rice, potatoes, beans and quinoa are vegan foods that are also an important part of meals.

Breakfast:
Vegans can eat quinoa and local fruit for their morning meal. Bananas and plantains are plentiful and make great breakfast foods with bread or grains.

Lunch/Dinner:

Peruvians do love their meat. Seafood dishes such as Ceviche or BBQ chicken are popular meals. In the highlands and villages, vegans should take note that cuy is served. It is a Peruvian guinea pig. Lomo Saltado, a popular beef stir fry can be found as a vegan version is some restaurants.

Vegans should feel comfortable in Peru, as certain grains and vegetables do play an important role in the cuisine. Most restaurants respect and prepare dishes for vegans. Soups such as yucca or tarwi are an important part of the meal also.

Italian influences include spaghetti dishes. Vegans can partake in this option, if the pasta is not made with eggs. The Italians also introduced pizza to this country.

Rice, beans, corn, potato dishes, and quinoa make excellent, vegan meal choices. Bananas, plantains, palm hearts, and yuca are also staples in the Peruvian vegan diet. Causa Limeña is a potato filled pastry.

Chinese restaurants, referred to as "Chifas" may also provide vegans with good dining options. Rocoto relleno is a stuffed pepper entrée which can be made vegan with quinoa and vegetables. Empanadas can be made with vegetables only also.

Fruit:

Chirimoya, camu camu, and lucuma are local fruits.

Beverages:

A couple of popular local beverages are chichi morada made from purple maiz and camu camu juice. Una de Gato or "cat's claw" tea is made from an Amazonian plant known for its healing properties.

Restaurants

Peru, in general can be vegan-friendly in most regions. The rice, corn, potato, bean, and quinoa staples are available for vegans. Lima has a few vegan-friendly restaurants, as do touristy areas such as Cuzco. The international vegetarian chain restaurant Govinda's in Cuzco serves traditional Peruvian food with a vegan twist.

Brazil

Like other South American countries, Brazilian cuisine is influenced by several cultures. Indigenous, Portuguese, Italian, Spanish, German, Asian, Arabic, and African immigrants played a part in developing the cuisine of Brazil.

Breakfast:

Bread and jam with fruit is common for the morning meal. Vegans can enjoy Acai na tigela which is an açaí mixture with bananas and granola. Coffee or tropical fruit juice such as papaya or mango are the common beverages.

Lunch/Dinner:

Meat along with rice and beans are common meal choices for Brazilians. Salads or empanadas may accompany the meal. Empanadas can be made vegan. Brazilian barbeque or churrasco is popular. However, vegans can partake in the side dishes of rice, potatoes, or polenta. Mandiocas and yams are also popular vegetables in Brazilian cooking. Veganism is not common here. When in a non-vegan restaurant, you need to verify that there is no seafood, chicken, pieces of meat or bone in the vegetable dish.

Some restaurants have a "food by the kilo" option which is great for vegans. You may select what you want from the buffet. Of course, vegetarian or vegan restaurants do not present this problem. The large cities should have enough dining options and veggie-friendly restaurants for vegans.

Pizza, pasta, and sushi (look for vegan) are Italian and Japanese influenced foods found in cities such as Sao Paolo. Snacks common in Brazil are Brazilian pine nuts called pinhão.

Fruits:

Acai is an anti-oxidant rich berry which grows in the Amazon. The juice is a wonderful beverage to serve with any vegan meal. Cupuaco is another Amazonian fruit which is commonly used in smoothies. Other tropical fruits such as mangoes, papayas, guavas, jackfruit, sapotes, jabuticabas, gaviolas, pitangas, cashews, carambolas, acerola, passionfruit are eaten raw or in juices.

Restaurants:

Rio and larger cities have several vegan restaurants. The remote regions will prove difficult for vegan travelers.

Chile

National dish: The national dish, porotos granados, for instance, has ingredients characteristic of Indian cooking (corn, squash, and beans).

The cuisine of Chile is influenced by local Indian peoples and European Spanish immigrants.

Breakfast:

Toasted bread with jelly or caramel manjar and either coffee or tea.

Lunch:

Beef or chicken is common along with a salad. Bean dishes are often served as sides. Vegans need just ask for a bean dish which is not cooked in lard or animal stock.

Once:

This is a light late afternoon/early evening meal of bread or sandwiches served with tea or coffee.

Dinner:

The late evening meal consists of meat, chicken or fish. Empanadas are popular snacks. They may be available in vegetable versions. Humitas are a boiled corn paste wrapped in corn husks. Porotos granados is a bean and squash stew which is vegan. There is a popular bean dish made with corn and pumpkin that may be a vegan option. Chickpeas, lentils and rice dishes are available for vegan meals.

Beverages:

Mote con huesillo is a local beverage made from wheat and sun-dried peaches.

Restaurants:

Santiago has a few vegan-friendly restaurants. The rest of the country may not have vegan dining.

Argentina

National dish: The Argentine national dish is parrilla which is a grilled mixture of steaks, sausage and organs, certainly not vegan. Beef and other meat is a huge part of Argentine cuisine.

The cuisine in this country is influenced by Spanish, Italian and French.

Breakfast:

Breakfast in Argentina consists of medialunas (croissants) with dulce de leche spread. Espresso coffee or yerba mate are the morning beverages. Churro pastries or tostada sandwiches are common also. The medialunas are typically made with butter or lard. Vegans should ask for regular bread or fruit instead.

Lunch/Dinner:

Although meat dishes are very popular in Argentina, there are some vegetable options. Vegetable pies and vegetable empanadas are common meals. Pizza and pasta dishes, as well as polenta are found in the Italian restaurants. Chinese and Japanese restaurants are common and may be a good vegan option. Vegetables such as potato, corn (in a loclo stew), pumpkin, palm hearts, eggplant, squash, and zucchini may be available side dishes for vegans. Quinoa and bean dishes are good choices for vegans too. Soy products are available in Argentina.

Beverages:

Yerba Mate tea or fresh fruit juices are popular beverages with the meals.

Restaurants:

Argentina is surprisingly vegan-friendly. Main cities such as Buenos Aires have several vegan restaurants. Even in some small villages (Bariloche and El Calafate), there are vegan options, as vegetables are plentiful here.

Ecuador

Meat, chicken, and seafood make up a large part of the meal in Ecuador. However, local vegetable dishes are available in large cities.

Breakfast:

Toast, sweet tamales, or tortillas are vegan options for breakfast in Ecuador. A plate of fruit or fresh fruit juice may accompany the meal.

Lunch/Dinner:

A vegan lunch can include a soup and a main dish with rice. Empanadas, humitas, or tamales filled with vegetables are common lunch or dinner foods. Good vegan main entrées include potato dishes, broccoli, palm hearts, yucca, corn, asparagus, yam, beans, lentils and fried plantains. Soup is also very popular in Ecuador. Choclo is barbequed corn, which is a popular snack.

Many restaurants offer veggie-friendly lunches. Soups are without doubt Ecuador's specialty. Quito, Otavalo, and Banos restaurants offer veggie options. In other towns, there may not be many vegan selections.

International cuisine is available in the capital of Quito. Visitors may dine at Chinese, Mexican, Italian, Indian, Japanese, or Arabic restaurants.

Beverages:

Local fruit juices such as naranjilla, tree tomato, mora, guanabana, maracuya and papaya can be found here.

Fruits:

Some common fruits grown in Ecuador are bananas, maracuya, guanabana, mangoes, papayas, and pineapples.

Restaurants:

The capital city of Quito has a few vegan-friendly restaurants, as does Guayaquil, Otavalo, and Banos. Other regions may prove difficult for vegans.

Bolivia

Meat, chicken, and seafood are eaten in quantity here. However, fruits and vegetables are plentiful also.

Breakfast:

Vegans may consume fruit salad for breakfast. Another vegan option in Ecuador are humitas which is corn meal wrapped inside a banana leaf then steamed.

Lunch/Dinner:

Potatoes, rice, and salad are popular vegan meal choices in Ecuador. Empanadas and humitas are also good choices whenever a vegan version is found.

Beverages:

Fresh fruit juices or api, which is a Bolivean tea, are common local beverages.

Restaurants:

There are just a few vegan-friendly restaurants in Bolivia.

Uruguay

Uruguayans consume a lot of beef. Seafood is also popular in this country. Since there is a large Italian influence, pizza and pasta are common foods here. Pizza is made without cheese. Great for vegans! Spain, France, and Germany also influenced the cuisine in Uruguay.

Breakfast:

For breakfast, toast and marmalade or pastries such as crepes are popular. Coffee or herbal, mate tea is the beverage of choice.

Lunch/Dinner:

Vegans may dine on pizza without cheese or pasta without eggs. Polenta dishes may be offered in restaurants also. Potatoes, rice, and corn are vegan options that may be found in restaurants. It is not a very veggie-centric culture.

Beverages:

Mate tea is a popular beverage in this country.

Restaurants

There are a few vegan-friendly restaurants in Uruguay.

Columbia

The cuisine of Columbia is influenced by indigenous peoples, Europeans, and Africans. There is a lot of meat, as well as pork, chicken, and fish consumed during meals. Vegans will be satisfied as there are several vegetables which are an important part of the Columbian diet.

Breakfast:

Breads or fruits, along with juice or coffee are decent vegan selections for breakfast in Columbia. Vegan tamales or arepas filled with corn or yucca are sometimes served for breakfast.

Lunch/Dinner:

Vegans in Columbia may dine on the region's vegetables including potatoes and cassava and grains such as corn and coconut rice. Lentils and peas are frequently consumed also. Rice and beans are sometimes cooked with lard in non-vegetarian restaurants.

Beverages:

Some popular beverages in Columbia are herbal teas, Columbian coffee, agua de panela sugar and water drink with lemon, salpicon diced fruit drink with soda, and champus which is made from corn, pineapple, and lulo

Fruit:

Columbia produces some wonderful tropical fruits such as zapote, lulo, curuba, mamoncillo, uchuva, feijoa, sweet granadilla, mamey, guama, tree tomato, chirimoya, guanabana, maracuya, mora, carambolo, guayabamanzana, sweet bananas , and pitahaya.

Restaurants:

There are quite a few vegan and vegan-friendly restaurants in Columbian cities.

Asia

Japan

Chinese culture influenced Japan's cuisine centuries ago. Important staples of the Japanese diet are rice, noodles, meat, fish, vegetables, and tofu. Vegans need to be careful, as fish sauce or dashi made with tuna may be included in the preparation of a vegetable dish. Fortunately, there are quite a few vegan restaurants all over Japan, so this should not be a problem.

Breakfast:

Rice is a typical breakfast food for the Japanese. Soybeans, pickled vegetables, rice porridge, or miso soup are also popular. The beverage of choice is green tea. These are all suitable choices for vegans.

Lunch/Dinner:

Rice, miso soup, and a vegetable dish with tofu make great vegan meals. Noodles, seaweed salad, or beans make good selections as main courses or side dishes. Some common vegetables used in Japanese cooking are mushrooms, eggplant, burdock, Chinese cabbage, sweet potato, and spinach.

Fruit:

The Japanese enjoy several kinds of fruits which grow locally. Some of these include chestnut, permission, kumquat, nashi pear, daidai, and yuzu.

Desserts:

Mochi is a sweet bean paste which is typically vegan. Rice cakes and any sweet made with green tea are popular. You may be able to find several types of vegan desserts.

Restaurants:

Japan is vegan-friendly. In non-vegan restaurants, vegans need to beware of fish stock in their meals. However, there are quite a few vegan restaurants in many cities.

China

This ancient culture has been around for centuries. Each region is known for its different cuisine. Cantonese and Szechuan cooking are most popular. Although meat, poultry, and fish play a major role in the Chinese diet, vegetables, noodles, and rice are important also. Vegans should find plenty of meal choices in China.

Breakfast:

For breakfast, the Chinese eat rice porridge, noodles, soybean milk soup, pancakes, pastries doughnuts, or buns.

Lunch/Dinner:

Rice dishes with green vegetables are a great vegan choice. Noodles, steamed filled-buns, green beans, eggplant, legumes, and bok choy are common foods that a vegan would eat in China. Steamed or stir-fried vegetables with soy sauce and a side of rice make wonderful entrees for vegans.

Beverages:

Tea is the preferred beverage. There are many kinds of Chinese herbal teas.

Fruit:

China produces many types of fruit including pears, apples, persimmons, melons, lychee, wolfberry, and kumquats.

Desserts:

Rice pudding, red bean cake, grass jelly, banana rolls, and pineapple buns are sweets that may be found in China. Some of these may be available in vegan versions.

Restaurants:

Vegan restaurants in China are plentiful in the cities.

Thailand

The cuisine of Thailand has been influenced by other Asian countries such as China, Malaysia, Vietnam, Laos, Cambodia, and Bhutan. Although fish and meat dishes are popular, vegetables are plentiful in the cooking. Vegans must be careful, as many dishes are prepared with shrimp or fish sauce.

Breakfast:

For breakfast, the Thai people will typically eat the same foods they consume at dinner time. Fried or steamed rice, porridge, or noodle soup may be eaten at breakfast time.

Lunch/Dinner:

Noodle dishes such as pad Thai, Italian, fried rice, or vegetable curries are good vegan meals.

Beverages:

Thai ice tea, durian juice, and Thai coffee are popular drinks in Thailand.

Fruit:

Thailand produces or consumes several exotic fruit such as durian, longan, dragonfruit, rambutan, custard apple, jujube, and sapodilla.

Restaurants:
There are many vegan and vegan-friendly restaurants in Bangkok, Chaing Mai, and Phuket regions of Thailand.

Malaysia

China, Thailand, and India influence the cuisine of Malaysia. Meat, fish, and chicken are eaten here in quantities. However, many rice, noodle, and vegetables dishes are common also.

Breakfast:

Roti pancakes (not vegan), breads filled with vegetables, and various rice dishes in coconut milk are popular breakfast foods. Vegans should ask if the roti or other breads are made with butter, ghee, or eggs.

Lunch/Dinner:

Rice, noodle, or vegetable curry dishes make wonderful vegan meals. It is important to verify that they were prepared without shrimp paste or fish sauce.

Beverages:

Some beverages which are popular in Malaysia are durian juice, coconut juice, and soybean milk with grass jelly.

Fruit:

Durian, lychee, longan, mangosteen, mango, and rambutan are the local fruits consumed in Thailand. They may be eaten raw or as juice or smoothies.

Desserts:

Rice noodles in coconut milk, chilled fruit (longan, rambutan), rice porridge, yam and sweet potato in coconut milk, and tapioca with banana in coconut milk are popular desserts.

Restaurants:

Malaysia appears to be very vegan-friendly. Many cities and villages have vegan dining options. The capital city of Kuala Lumpur and Penang have many vegan restaurants.

Indonesia

The cuisine of Indonesia is influenced by the local indigenous peoples, India, the Middle East, China and several Europe countries including Spain, Portugal, and the Dutch. While seafood, chicken and fish are common in the cuisine, rice is also a staple as are vegetables. Creamy, milky dishes are more than likely vegan, coconut milk-based. However, vegans need to verify that the popular peanut sauce does not contain fish broth.

Breakfast:

Fried rice, fried noodles, vegetable porridge are the common breakfast foods. Vegans should ask for rice or noodles without egg on top.

Lunch/Dinner:

Tofu, tempeh, rice, and noodles make up the vegan main entrees. The meals typically consist of rice, soup, salad, sambal, and vegetable dishes. Some of the vegetables which are commonly eaten here include palm flour, sweet potatoes and cassava, mustard greens, mung beans, cabbage, cauliflower, carrots, string beans, potatoes and corn.

Fruit:

One may find the typical tropical fruits here such as rambutan, mango, durian, jackfruit, coconut, and bananas.

Beverages:

Tea, coffee, and various juices such as guava, soursop, and mango are popular. Fruit shakes and hot beverages are common also.

Desserts:

Ginger beverages, grass jelly, coconut, pumpkin, seaweed, and azuki beans are considered desserts.

Restaurants:

Bali is very vegan-friendly and several islands have some vegan restaurants serving local, Asian cuisine. Various vegetables, rice, noodles, and fruits are plentiful in the cuisine.

Singapore

Malaysia, China, India, and Indonesia have influenced the cuisine of this country. Some of these cultures do not eat pork or beef. However, meat is eaten here. Vegans can find lots of vegetable, rice, and nodle dishes. They need just beware of ghee in the Indian entrees or fish sauce in the other Asian meals. Hawker stalls or food courts contain multiple restaurants serving the cuisines of the aforementioned cultures. Vegetarian hawker stalls are becoming more popular.

Breakfast:

Rice cakes, fried vermicelli noodles(no egg), rice cooked in coconut milk, Roti paratha pancakes, pastries bean curd, rice porridge, or bean soup are common breakfast foods.

Vegans should not consume kaya toast as it is made with eggs.

Lunch/Dinner:

Fried rice dishes, noodles, leafy green vegetables, mixed vegetable dishes, and Indian vegetable curries make for great vegan options.

Fruit:

Rambutan, jackfruit, mangosteen, longan, lychee, and pineapple are great exotic fruits one may find in Singapore.

Beverages:

Bubble teas, ginger tea, soy bean milk, sugar cane juice, and durian shakes are delicious beverages that are commonly served here.

Desserts:

Vegans can delight in desserts here, as beans and fruit are commonly used in sweets over ice or in coconut milk.

Restaurants:

Singapore has many vegan and vegan-friendly restaurants, including options at their many hawker stall food courts.

Vietnam

Chinese immigrants and French settlers have influenced the cuisine of Vietnam. While fish and meat are important staples in the Vietnamese diet, it is a very vegan-friendly country also.

Breakfast:

Pho noodle soup, sticky rice, French bread, or tropical fruit(mangoes, bananas) are good vegan breakfast foods. Vegans should make sure that the pho does not contain meat or fish broth.

Lunch/Dinner:

Boiled rice, sticky rice, rice cakes, fried rice, pho noodles, soup, vegetable dumplings, pickled or steamed vegetables, vermicelli, and spring rolls are common Vietnamese meal choices. Vegans should verify they are not cooked with animal stock, lard, fish sauce or contain meat or seafood. Commonly served vegetable dishes may include bok choy, carrots, bitter melon, cabbage, eggplant, jicama, and cauliflower.

Fruits:

Acerola, Buddha's hand, cannistel, cherimoya, coconut, custard apple, durian, guava, jackfruit, longan, rambutan, mango, mangosteen, pitaya, papaya, and lychee are exotic fruits which are popular in Vietnam.

Beverages:
Coffee, sugarcane juice, pennywort juice, and a soybean milk drink are popular beverages in this country.

Desserts:

Sweet sticky rice and beans, fried bananas, chilled fruit such as longan or rambutan are favorite desserts. These are vegan.

Restaurants:

Vietnam is vegan-friendly. There are many vegan restaurants in several, touristy cities. In addition, rice, noodle, and vegetable dishes are an important part of the cuisine.

Cambodia

France, Thailand and China have had an influence on Cambodian cooking. While fish and beef are popular, vegans may take comfort in partaking in the many noodle or rice dishes common here.

Breakfast:

French baguette bread, Noodle soup or rice porridge dishes are eaten for breakfast. Vegans should ask for versions which are not cooked in chicken stock.

Lunch/Dinner:

Rice noodles, rice cakes filled with bananas, and vegetable stir fries are good vegan choices for lunch or dinner. Stir fry dishes usually include vegetables such as Chinese broccoli, snow peas, bok choy, cabbage, baby corn, snow peas, and mushrooms. Squash dishes can be cooked, stir fried, or steamed. Vegetable soups can be made with bitter melons, beans, or luffa.

Fruits:

Fruits that one may find in Cambodia include mangosteen, papaya, sapodilla, durian, kuy, pineapple, palmyra, jackfruit, watermelon, banana, coconut, rambutan, watermelon, star apple, and rose apple.

Beverages:

Fruit shakes such as durian, banana, or mango are popular.

Desserts:

Sticky rice and jackfruit wrapped in banana leaves is a great vegan dessert.

Restaurants:

Cambodia is not known for vegan dining. There are just a couple of vegetarian restaurants in the capital which serve vegan entrees. Vegans may have difficulty dining in this country, as dishes contain meat, poultry, fish, animal broth, or fish sauce.

Tibet

Tibetan cuisine does not really borrow from its neighbors, as only certain foods such as grains and rice grow at this high altitude. Larger cities may serve some Chinese food. Meats are very commonly eaten. Vegans may find some vegetable soups, veggie burgers, rice dishes, and vegetables.

Breakfast:

Tibetan breads with chickpea and potato stew are vegan breakfast items one may find here.

Lunch/Dinner:

Vegetable steamed momos, tingmo bread, vegetable soups, veggie burgers, barley, noodles, or potato stew.

Fruits:

Goji berries grow in the Himalayas.

Beverages:

Tibetan tea is not vegan as it contains yak milk and butter. Vegans may drink Chinese jasmine tea.

Restaurants:

There are no vegan restaurants in the region. Vegans may have difficulty finding meals at times. However, there are some vegetable dishes and breads which are suitable. Chinese cuisine restaurants may have better vegan offerings.

Nepal

India, China, Tibet influence the cuisine of Nepal.

Breakfast:

A typical Nepalese breakfast may include bread, vegetables, and a soup. Tea is a beverage of choice.

Lunch/Dinner:

There are many vegetables and grains commonly eaten in Nepal. Vegans may dine on grain dishes made with barley, millet, or fried rice or lentil beans. Popular vegetable dishes containing potatoes, corn, vegetable samosas, spinach, green beans, cauliflower, cabbage, squash, curried vegetables, potatoes with bamboo shoots, vegetable soup, and green vegetables are good choices for vegans also.

Fruits:

Mango, papaya, jackfruit, bananas, mandarin oranges, and asian pears are popular fruits in Nepal.

Beverages:

Tea, sugarcane juice, and a fermented millet drink are popular beverages in Nepal.

Restaurants

There is only one vegan restaurant and a few vegan-friendly restaurants in the capital city of Kathmandu. It may not be difficult to find vegan dining options in restaurants, as rice, grains, soups, veggie burgers, and vegetables are a part of the Nepalese cuisine.

India

Europe, western Asia, and Iran have influenced the cuisine of India. Although certain meats are eaten in India, there are certainly lots of rice, bean, and vegetable dishes for vegans. It is important to make sure to ask for dishes without ghee (clarified butter).

Breakfast:

In each region of India, one may find different foods served for breakfast. Vegetable-filled pakoras, sambar soup, vegetable-filled dosas, and utthappam vegetable pancakes are eaten in various areas of the north, south, east, and west.

Lunch/Dinner:

Rice, lentils, chickpeas, mung beans, bean soups, veggie burgers, and vegetable curries are great meal choices for vegans. Vegetable samosas can be eaten as a snack or appetizer.

Fruits:

Guava, banana, cashew fruit, noni, neem, sapota are fruits commonly grown in India.

Beverages:

Masala chai tea or mango juice are popular Indian beverages which are served with a typical meal.

Restaurants:

It is difficult to find vegan restaurants in India, as a lot of recipes call for ghee, clarified butter. There are many vegetarian restaurants on the other hand. The best bets for vegans would be to travel with a veggie-friendly travel agency or to ask vegetarian restaurants if they could make any ingredient substitutions.

Africa

Morocco

Moroccan cuisine is influenced by Moors, Berbers, African, Arab, and Mediterranean peoples. Beef and lamb are food staples. However, Couscous is also a common choice.

Breakfast:

Tea, bread with marmalade, bissara (a split pea soup) are popular breakfast items for vegans. However, it is important to verify that the stock or broth is not of animal origin.

Lunch/Dinner:

Couscous, vegetable tagine stew, lentil soup, and Harira(a soup made with tomatoes, beans, lentils and other items) are good choices for vegan diners. Vegans should ask the waiter if the soup contains an animal based broth. Salads containing eggplant and tomato are common in a Moroccan meal. Eggplant turnovers served with tomato, rice, lentils and saffron rice may be vegan also.

Fruits:

Peaches, pears, cherries, and watermelons are popular Moroccan fruits based on season.

Beverages:

Green tea with mint is the popular beverage. Fruit juices such as orange juice may be served with breakfast.

Restaurants:

Marrakesch and Tangier each have one vegan-friendly restaurant. Vegan diners must be careful what to order as many of the restaurants use chicken stock in their couscous. Vegetable tagines may be the best bet. It is suggested to speak with waiters regarding the options and if the chef can omit the animal stock or dairy.

Tunisia

The cuisine takes its influences from Mediterranean and native Berber peoples. Fish, lamb, and game are highly popular. Vegans may find little more than couscous dishes. It needs to be verified as to whether or not the dish contains meat pieces or a chicken broth.

Breakfast:

Nuts, fruits, pastries, cereals, chickpea soup, dates, and bread with jam are some vegan breakfast foods you may find in Tunisia.

Lunch/Dinner:

Vegans should beware that tagines in Tunisia are made with eggs. Couscous may be an option if it is not made with animal stock or meat. Chakchouka is a vegetable dish similar to ratatouille. However, vegans should ask for it without the egg on top. Popular vegetables such as stuffed tomatoes, potatoes, peppers, eggplants, squash and turnip are grilled.

Fruit:

Dates, oranges, and lemons are eaten as snacks or as part of salads.

Beverages:

Orange juice, lemon juice, and mint tea are common beverages.

Vegan-Friendly Restaurants:

There are no vegan-friendly restaurants listed under the popular vegan resource sites online. However, vegans may find couscous dishes, grilled vegetables, or Italian pasta dishes. It is wise to verify with a waiter that nothing has been cooked in dairy or a meat or chicken-based broth.

Ghana

The various ethnic tribes from each region are the contributing factor to the cuisine of the country. Fish and meat are staples. However, there are some starchy vegetables and rices which play an important role also.

Breakfast:

Bread, cornmeal porridge, sweet bread, and tea are popular breakfast items.

Lunch/Dinner:

Rice and beans, fufu (mashed cassava and plantain or yam), okra stew and various other rice or cassava dishes make great vegan meals.

Fruit:

Pineapples, coconuts and oranges are the commonly eaten fruits in Ghana.

Beverages:

Orange juice, pineapple juice, coconut juice, and tea are local beverages you may find served with meals.

Restaurants:

Ghana is a seafood loving country. However, there are two vegan restaurants here, one being in the touristy capital of Accra. A couple of restaurants along the coast offer vegan-friendly meals and soy smoothies.

Kenya

Kenya's cuisine has been influenced by Great Britain and East India. Game drives produce a culture which thrives on exotic meats. However, the local cuisine does have some popular vegetable dishes, as well as dishes famous from the cuisine of India.

Breakfast:

Ugali is a Kenyan breakfast dish made with cornmeal or millet. It may be served with m'baazi (mashed peapods). Other breakfast foods include black-eyed peas, bananas, and yams, mandazi (fried dough), or a bean and corn stew.

Lunch/Dinner:

Stews are popular meals. Kenyans also like vegan dishes such as sweet potatoes, bananas, and plantains, with rice, millet, corn, and irio (greens, beans, and corn). Other popular vegan dishes are stewed beans, roasted corn, and githeri (corn and beans). Most meals include sukuma wiki. This is a collard greens entrée. Chapati (Indian flat bread) or samosas, may be served with potatoes or other vegetables.

Fruit:

Bananas, pineapples, and papaya, as well as other citrus fruits are popular.

Beverages:

Tea, passion fruit juice and other fresh fruit juices are popular in Kenya.

Restaurants:

Although there are not many vegan restaurants in Kenya, vegans should not have a problem with dining, as there are many Indian influenced, vegetable dishes in the cuisine here.

Tanzania

The British, Germans, Indians, Arabs, and local tribes have all influenced the cuisine of Tanzania. It is a country where the meat produced from game drives is commonly eaten. There are a few vegan meal options available here.

Breakfast:

For breakfast, a vegan in Tanzania may chose to eat fruits such as pineapples, sweet bananas, avocados, and mangoes or cooked root vegetables. Mandaji, a fried bread, donut-like item can be made vegan without milk or egg.

Lunch/Dinner:

For main meals, vegan can select from a variety of dishes including coconut bean soup, rice(wali), ugali (maize porridge),chapati (Indian bread), or biryani rice. Other popular vegetables are okra, spinach, green peas, beans and cassava.

Fruit:

Sweet bananas, mangos, pineapples, plantains, avocados are some of the local fruit.

Beverages:

Teas, pineapple, orange, or sugar cane juices are the popular beverages in Tanzania.

Restaurants:

Although there is only one vegan-friendly restaurant in the main town, vegans can dine on the many Indian rice and vegetable dishes popular in the country.

South Africa

The cuisine of South Africa has been influenced by the local indigenous peoples, the British colonists, and the Cape Malay slaves from southeast Asia (the Bengal region of India, Indonesia and Malaysia). Later in its history, other settlers from Europe (Portuguese, French, German, Dutch) colonized the region and influenced its foods. The Cape Malay food is the most vegan-friendly, as it has a lot of Indian curry dishes in its repertoire. Many ethnic restaurants can be found in South Africa also including Chinese, Japanese, West African, and Moroccan. This gives a vegan many choices.

Breakfast:

Oat, sorghum, and oat porridges are common breakfast foods. Fresh fruit is a good vegan option. American and British breakfast items such as cold cereals have become a part of the culture also. Tofu scramble can be found on the menu of vegan-friendly restaurants in large cities such as Cape Town.

Lunch/Dinner:

Cape Malay vegetable curry is a delicious vegan entree. South African vegetable stews can be prepared vegan at various restaurants. The other vegan options include Ethiopian vegetable stew or one of many other cuisines served at the plentiful ethnic restaurants in the region.

Fruit:

Apricots, peaches, melons, pears are grown in this country. Tropical fruits such as bananas, pineapples, and mangoes grow in some regions.

Beverages:

Roobois tea and aloe ferox juice are local beverages that one should try in South Africa.

Restaurants:

South Africa is very vegan-friendly in the large cities such as Cape Town and Johannesburg. There are many international cuisine restaurants such as Indian dining establishments which serve vegan options.

Egypt

The cuisine has been influenced by its ancient history. Fortunately for vegans, it does consist of many vegetable and bean dishes.

Breakfast:

Ful madams (fava beans cooked in olive oil and herbs) with pita bread is a great vegan breakfast food.

Lunch/Dinner:

Stuffed vegetables with rice, grape leaves, falafel, baba ghanoush, ful madames (mashed fava beans), and moussaka(an eggplant dish) are typical vegan entrees. North African vegetable tagines can be found on restaurant menus also. Pita bread is served with many delicious condiments and hummus spreads.

Fruit:

Apples, guavas, bananas, dates, oranges, melon, peaches, plums, and grapes are grown in Egypt.

Beverages:

Two kinds of local, black tea or hibiscus tea are beverages to try here in Egypt.

Restaurants:

There is only one vegan-friendly restaurant in Cairo. However, ful madames is an extremely popular dish which vegans will not have a problem finding at restaurants throughout the region. In other parts of the country, such as Luxor restaurants are sometimes willing to prepare a vegetable tagine or serve hummus and pita bread for vegans. Northern African entrees such as vegetable tagine stews, felafel, or baba ghanoush can be found at many restaurants also.

Botswana

The cuisine in Botswana is influenced only by its own tribal people. However, it shares some dishes with other south African nations. Meat is a large part of the cuisine. Grains and a wide variety of vegetables are grown plentifully here also.

Breakfast:

Porridge made of grains such as sorghum or maize is a popular breakfast food.

Lunch/Dinner:

Sorghum and maize are the main, local crops. Wheat and rice are popular. Many bean varieties grow in Botswana. Peanuts are also grown here. Some locally grown vegetables include spinach, potatoes, onions, carrots, cabbage, tomatoes, sweet potatoes and lettuce.

Fruit:

A local fruit called marula, watermelon, and lerotse melon are plentiful.

Beverages:

Soft drinks and ginger beer are common drinks.

Restaurants:

No vegan-friendly restaurants listed. It is not a vegan-friendly restaurant scene. However, vegans can look for the main staple crops and veggies at local restaurants.

Namibia

The cuisine in Namibia has German influences, as well as local, tribal influences. Vegans beware if you are offered food without knowing what it is. It is very common to eat worms in Namibia!

Breakfast:

Corn or millet porridge is a good vegan choice for breakfast.

Lunch/Dinner:

Some vegan options for meals include rice, pasta and locally grown crops such as cabbage, asparagus, or potatoes. Fruits and nuts are popular ingredients in the meals. Mushroom soup is popular also.

Fruit:

Dates and grapes grow here.

Beverages:

The country is not known for any particular fruit juice or tea.

Restaurants:

This safari country is not very vegan-friendly. There is only one vegan-friendly restaurant in the city.

Zimbabwe

The local tribes and also the British have influenced the cuisine in this country. Vegans should be careful not to eat everything they are offered. Worms and bugs are common snacks here.

Breakfast:

Bota, a thin porridge made of cornmeal served with peanut butter or jam. Vegans should verify that their bota is not made with milk or butter.

Lunch/Dinner:

Squash, corn, yams, pumpkins, peanuts are just some of the vegetables that vegans will find in meals. Nhedzi soup is made with wild mushrooms. Sadza is a very popular, thick porridge. It is served with beans, or green vegetables such as collard greens or spinach. Beans may be included in dinner selections also.

Fruit:

Papaya is popular here.

Beverages:

Mazoe is a kind of orange juice which is a popular beverage. Tea is common also, as the British influence is felt.

Restaurants:

There is only one vegan-friendly restaurant in Zimbabwe. The country offers a good choice of restaurants which serve International dishes beside Zimbabwe cuisines.

Europe

England

Other European countries such as France and Italy have made an impact on the cuisine, as well as China and India. England is known to be a haven for vegetarians and vegans.

Breakfast:

Vegans can eat a breakfast consisting of tofu scramble, cereal with soymilk, toast, and orange juice or porridge in the winter. Vegan muffins, waffles, and donuts are not difficult to find in the UK either.

Lunch/Dinner:

Boiled vegetables, veggie burgers, Chinese stir fry, and Indian curries are popular dishes for vegans. Two vegetables are usually served at meals, including potatoes. Rice and pasta are also popular dishes served.

Beverages:

High Tea in the afternoon is a British tradition. Earl Grey and English Breakfast Tea are two of the more popular choices.

Restaurants:

London has many vegan restaurants. It is a very vegan-friendly place. Brighton suburb, about an hour away is a mecca for vegan dining.

Scotland

Scottish cuisine is similar to the English. Fruits and vegetable dishes have become more common, as have Indian, Thai, Italian, and Chinese foods.

Breakfast:

A typical western breakfast of cereal with soymilk is a good vegan option. There are also shops in Edinburgh which sell vegan donuts. Vegan muffins, scones, waffles and other typical western breakfast items can be found in vegan cafes.

Lunch/Dinner:

Vegan versions of the popular Scottish "Haggis" dish are available at vegan restaurants. In Edinburgh, there is a vegan-friendly baked potato shop. The international dining scene is popular so one may find vegan versions of Thai, Italian, Indian, and Chinese meals. Vegetable dishes, veggie burgers, rice, and pasta are good vegan options too.

Restaurants:

Edinburgh has several vegan-friendly restaurants. Glasgow has quite a few vegan restaurants.

Ireland

Ireland is a meat and potatoes country. However, vegan food can be found easily enough at several restaurants in the capital and other cities.

Breakfast:

A typical Western breakfast includes cereal with soymilk, oatmeal, tofu scramble, waffles, pastries or scones.

Lunch/Dinner:

Typical Western sandwiches, soups, veggie burgers, beans, noodle dishes, tofu and vegetable entrees with rice, or international meals such as Thai, Italian, Chinese, or Indian curries.

Restaurants:

Ireland has several vegan-friendly restaurants in Dublin and in its other cities and towns.

Iceland

Iceland is a seafood-centric country. Vegan food is not popular at all in the countryside. However, it is possible to find some in the capital of Reykjavik.

Breakfast:

A Western vegan breakfast includes cereal with soymilk, juice and toast with jam. Some cafes may serve tofu scramble.

Lunch/Dinner:

Western meals including noodle dishes, tofu and vegetables, rice, soups, veggie burgers, beans and international dishes are the norm here for vegans.

Restaurants:

Iceland is non-vegan in the countryside. Eating fish is the norm here. However, the capital city of Rekyjavik has a handful of vegan-friendly restaurants. Several cafes also serve vegan desserts and ice cream.

Finland

Finland is a seafood-centric country. Vegan food is not very popular. However, it is possible to find some vegan-friendly restaurants in the capital and a few in the suburbs.

Breakfast:

A typical Western breakfast includes cereal with soymilk or fruit as a good vegan option.

Lunch/Dinner:

Typical Western sandwiches, soups, veggie burgers, beans, noodle dishes, tofu and vegetable entrees with rice, or international meals such as Thai, Italian, Chinese, or Indian curries.

Restaurants:

There are several vegan-friendly restaurants in Helsinki and a few in the suburbs.

Norway

Norway is a seafood-centric country. Vegan food is not very popular. However, it is possible to find some vegan-friendly restaurants in the capital and a few in the suburbs.

Breakfast:

A typical Western breakfast including cereal with soymilk or fruit is a good vegan option.

Lunch/Dinner:

Typical Western sandwiches, soups, veggie burgers, beans, noodle dishes, tofu and vegetable entrees with rice, or international meals such as Thai, Italian, Chinese, or Indian curries.

Restaurants:

There are a couple of vegan restaurants in the capital and several vegan-friendly ones. Throughout the country, there are a few scattered vegan-friendly restaurants.

Sweden

Sweden is a seafood-centric country. Vegan food is not very popular. However, it is possible to find some vegan-friendly restaurants in the capital and a few in the suburbs.

Breakfast:

Typical Western breakfast including cereal with soymilk or fruit is a good vegan option.

Lunch/Dinner:

Typical Western sandwiches, soups, veggie burgers, beans, noodle dishes, tofu and vegetable entrees with rice, or international meals such as Thai, Italian, Chinese, or Indian curries.

Restaurants:

There are a couple of vegan restaurants in the capital and several vegan-friendly ones. Throughout the country, there are a few scattered vegan-friendly restaurants. It is also possible to find vegan desserts and vegan ice cream. There is even an all-vegan grocery shop called "GoodStore".

Netherlands

The Netherlands is very vegan-friendly. Amsterdam has many vegan restaurants and shops

Breakfast:

A typical Western breakfast includes cereal with soymilk, oatmeal, muffins, waffles, pancakes, pastries or scones.

Lunch/Dinner:

Typical Western sandwiches, soups, veggie burgers, beans, noodle dishes, tofu and vegetable entrees with rice, or international meals such as Thai, Italian, Chinese, or Indian curries.

Restaurants:

This is a very vegan-friendly country! There are several vegan restaurants in the capital and several vegan-friendly ones. Throughout the country, there are a few scattered vegan-friendly restaurants. It is also possible to find vegan desserts and vegan ice cream.

Belgium

Belgium is fairly vegan-friendly in the capital and a couple of other towns.

Breakfast:

A typical Western breakfast includes cereal with soymilk or fruit.

Lunch/Dinner:

Typical Western sandwiches, soups, veggie burgers, beans, noodle dishes, tofu and vegetable entrees with rice, or international meals such as Thai, Italian, Chinese, or Indian curries.

Restaurants:

This is a vegan-friendly country! There are several vegan restaurants in the capital and several vegan-friendly ones. Brussels, Brugge, Antwerp, and Ghent offer good, vegan dining. Throughout the country, there are a few scattered vegan-friendly restaurants. It is also possible to find vegan desserts and vegan ice cream.

Denmark

Denmark is not the easiest place for vegans to dine. However, there are a few vegan-friendly places in the capital and a couple of other towns.

Breakfast:

A typical Western breakfast includes cereal with soymilk, oatmeal, muffins, waffles, pancakes, Danish pastries, croissants, or scones.

Lunch/Dinner:

Typical Western sandwiches, soups, veggie burgers, beans, noodle dishes, tofu and vegetable entrees with rice, or international meals such as Thai, Italian, Chinese, or Indian curries.

Restaurants:

Being vegan is a challenge in Denmark. There are a few vegan-friendly restaurants in the capital and a couple of them in the suburbs. The capital of Copenhagen has one raw food, vegan restaurant, in addition to a bakery which sells some vegan Danish pastries.

Italy

Italy is known for its various pasta dishes and pizza. However, it is also suitable for vegans, as vegan versions of pasta and pizza can be found.

Breakfast:

A typical Western breakfast including cereal with soymilk or fruit is a good vegan option.

Lunch/Dinner:

Vegan pasta varieties and pizza are the popular choices here. Vegan cheese is substituted on pizza.

Restaurants:

There are quite a few vegan and vegan-friendly restaurants in the capital of Rome, including raw food restaurants. One can find a few vegan-friendly dining establishments in other cities. Vegan desserts, ice cream, and Italian gelato can be found here also.

France

France is not well-known for vegan dining. However, it is very easy for vegans to find great meals in Paris.

Breakfast:

A typical Western breakfast includes cereal with soymilk, oatmeal, muffins, waffles, pancakes, pastries, croissants, or scones. France is known for its croissants and crepes. Several shops sell the vegan versions.

Lunch/Dinner:

Typical Western sandwiches, soups, veggie burgers, beans, noodle dishes, tofu and vegetable entrees with rice, or international meals such as Thai, Italian, Chinese, or Indian curries.

Restaurants:

Paris has half a dozen vegan restaurants and several vegan-friendly ones. There are a few vegan-friendly restaurants scattered throughout the country, though not common.

Germany

Germany is typically thought of as a meat-loving country. Vegans will be pleasantly surprised about all of the vegan restaurants, desserts, bakeries, ice creameries, and grocery shops that offer tons of vegan options, especially in Berlin!

Breakfast:

A typical Western breakfast includes cereal with soymilk, oatmeal, muffins, waffles, or pancakes. Vegan bakeries offer pastries, croissants, or scones.

Lunch/Dinner:

Typical Western sandwiches, soups, veggie burgers, beans, noodle dishes, tofu and vegetable entrees with rice, or international meals such as Thai, Italian, Chinese, or Indian curries. A typical German meat dish can be found as its vegan counterpart "Seitanwurst" or a vegan hotdog with "Currywurst".

Restaurants:

Munich has a couple of vegan restaurants, while Berlin has dozens of them. There are many vegan-friendly restaurants scattered all over the country. There are many shops which offer vegan pastries, cupcakes, and ice cream.

Austria

Austria is mainly a meat-loving nation. There are not many vegan-friendly restaurants.

Breakfast:

A typical Western breakfast including cereal with soymilk or fruit is good for vegan travelers. Vegan versions of oatmeal, muffins, waffles, pancakes, pastries, croissants, or scones may be found at vegan-friendly restaurants.

Lunch/Dinner:

Typical Western sandwiches, soups, veggie burgers, beans, noodle dishes, tofu and vegetable entrees with rice, or international meals such as Thai, Italian, Chinese, or Indian curries.

Restaurants:

Vienna has two vegan restaurants from the international chain called "Loving Hut". There are a few vegan-friendly restaurants. However, most of them are Indian or Chinese, not typical Austrian fare. Salzburg has a few vegan-friendly restaurants offering European fare and vegan desserts.

Poland

Poland is a carnivorous country. However, it is not very difficult for vegans to find decent meals.

Breakfast:

A typical Western breakfast includes cereal with soymilk, oatmeal, muffins, waffles, pancakes, pastries, croissants, or scones. Poland is known for its croissants and crepes. Several shops sell the vegan versions.

Lunch/Dinner:

Typical Western sandwiches, soups, veggie burgers, beans, noodle dishes, tofu and vegetable entrees with rice, or international meals such as Thai, Italian, Chinese, or Indian curries. Pierogi is a popular Polish dish.

Local favorites such as Schnitzel (they have a soy version) or potato salad are offered at vegan-friendly cafes.

Restaurants:

There is one vegan restaurant in the capital of Warsaw and several vegan-friendly restaurants both in Warsaw and Krakow, serving European and Asian foods.

Russia

Russian is very meat-centric and seafood-loving. It is very difficult to find vegan food.

Breakfast:

Typical Western breakfast including cereal with soymilk is the best choice for vegan travelers. There do not appear to be many options for vegan pastries.

Lunch/Dinner:

Typical Western sandwiches, soups, veggie burgers, beans, noodle dishes, tofu and vegetable entrees with rice, or international meals such as Thai, Italian, Chinese, or Indian curries.

Restaurants:

Moscow has only one vegan-friendly restaurant and just a handful of vegan-friendly places. St. Petersburg does not have any vegan restaurants but has a few vegan-friendly establishments. The remainder of the country is not vegan-friendly. It appears that the vegan-friendly restaurants serve typical Western meals, not Russian food. There seems to be only one or two restaurants in St. Petersburg that serve veggie-friendly, Russian fare.

Greece

Grecian meals involve a lot of meat and fish. Although there a lot of vegetable side dishes and bean soups, there are not many vegan-friendly restaurants in the country.

Breakfast:

Typical Western breakfast including cereal with soymilk(if it can be found) or fruit.

Lunch/Dinner:

Typical Western sandwiches, soups, beans, rice dishes, and vegetable entrees are good vegan selections. Popular vegetable side dishes are spinach, chicory, endives, potato, and lima beans. Lentil soups are common too.

Restaurants:

There are just a couple of vegan-friendly restaurants in Athens and other towns. The best bet is probably to ask a non-veggie friendly restaurant if they could prepare some vegetables for you without using animal products. As Greeks love leafy green vegetables with olive oil, eggplant, zucchini, bean dishes, and rice, this should not be a problem for anyone.

Spain

Spanish meals are very centered around meat. However, vegans can find many dining establishments here that will cater to them.

Breakfast:

A typical Western breakfast including cereal with soymilk or fruit. Vegan pastries may be found in some cafes.

Lunch/Dinner:

Typical Western sandwiches, soups, veggie burgers, beans, noodle dishes, tofu and vegetable entrees with rice, or international meals such as Thai, Italian, Chinese, or Indian curries.

Restaurants:

Madrid and Barcelona have a couple of vegan restaurants. In addition, they have quite a few vegan-friendly restaurants there. Most serve international cuisine such as Indian or Asian. One can find some vegan-friendly restaurants scattered across the country, though not everywhere.

Portugal

Most Portuguese meals involve meat or fish. There are not many typical vegetable dishes.

Breakfast:

A typical Western breakfast including cereal with soymilk or fruit is the best vegan breakfast option. There are not many vegan-friendly bakeries in Portugal. Some of the vegan-friendly restaurants do serve vegan desserts.

Lunch/Dinner:

Typical Western sandwiches, soups, veggie burgers, beans, noodle dishes, tofu and vegetable entrees with rice, or international meals such as Thai, Italian, Chinese, or Indian curries.

Restaurants:

There is one vegan restaurant and about a dozen vegan-friendly restaurants in the capital city of Lisbon. Most serve international Asian or Indian fare. One or two restaurants serve the vegan version of popular Portuguese dishes. There are a few scattered vegan-friendly restaurants throughout the country, though not that common to find.

Eastern Europe (Romania/Hungary/Czech Republic)

Eastern European countries are known to not be very vegan-friendly. There are some vegan-friendly restaurants in these countries, however.

Breakfast:

A typical Western breakfast including cereal with soymilk or fruit is the best vegan breakfast option. Bread with tomatoes and cucumbers or other veggies is a common breakfast in this region also. There are not many vegan-friendly bakeries in this region of Eastern Europe. Some of the vegan-friendly restaurants do serve vegan desserts.

Lunch/Dinner:

Typical Western sandwiches, soups, veggie burgers, beans, noodle dishes, tofu and vegetable entrees with rice, or international meals such as Thai, Italian, Chinese, or Indian curries.

Restaurants:

Romania has a couple of vegan-friendly restaurants serving international cuisine in the capital city of Bucharest. Both Hungary and the Czech Republic have a few vegan restaurants and several vegan-friendly restaurants which serve local and international cuisine.

Summary

As you can see, vegan travelers typically have great meal options in many parts of the world. The international, vegan dining scene is an amazing cornucopia of delicious meals, tasty desserts, and refreshing beverages with more options to come in the future!

It is fairly easy to find vegan restaurants or options almost anywhere in the world. I found great vegan meals in Argentina cattle country, South African safari region, Brazil's land of barbeque, and in seafood-loving Iceland!

I hope that the travel tips and dining information in this guide will provide you with positive incentives to start exploring our wonderfully vegan-friendly, breathtakingly beautiful world!

Happy and delicious travels to everyone!

14453751R00128

Made in the USA
Lexington, KY
01 April 2012